Friends and Relations

Using Literature with Social Themes K–2

Carol Otis Hurst
and Rebecca Otis

SMALL
·B·O·O·K·
SERIES

10,00

All net proceeds from the sale of *Friends and Relations: Using Literature with Social Themes K–2* support the work of Northeast Foundation for Children, a nonprofit educational organization whose mission is to foster safe, challenging, and joyful elementary classrooms and schools.

13-digit ISBN: 978-1-89298-902-4
10-digit ISBN: 1-89298-902-6

Library of Congress catalog card number 99-60684

Second printing April 2005

Photographs: Peter Wrenn, Cherry Wyman, Marlynn K. Clayton, Apple Lord

Cover and book design: Woodward Design

Northeast Foundation for Children
85 Avenue A, Suite 204
P.O. Box 718
Turners Falls, MA 01376-0718
800-360-6332

www.responsiveclassroom.org

Table of Contents

Foreword
A Note From the Publisher

ALL OF THE LITERATURE recommended in *Friends and Relations* explores social relationships.

One of the underpinnings of the Responsive Classroom approach to teaching is the belief that social interaction provides the most fertile ground for cognitive growth. Great learning, of course, also takes place in moments of solitude, individual contemplation and reflection, but we humans are social beings, after all, and our motivation to learn and the context in which we learn reflects that.

We also believe that knowing the children we teach is as important as knowing the content we teach. Knowledge of our children—individual, cultural and developmental knowledge—should inform our decisions about classrooms and curriculum. There are certain patterns of development indicative of particular ages. Knowing them can help us understand our students and enrich our conversations with them.

Below are some general developmental trends to consider as you use this book. These are trends which have relevance to the five themes in *Friends and Relations*: friendship; bullies, pests, and teasing; isolation and reaching out across generations; families; and working together. You may want to refer back to these comments about development as you read the books in these sections and think about them with your students.

Please do remember, however, that children are first and foremost individuals. Some are shy and some are bold, regardless of what age they are. Situations arise and circumstances exist in their lives which affect children profoundly. As Chip Wood emphasizes in *Yardsticks: Children in the Classroom Ages 4–14,* developmental considerations are "general expectations that help us gain an appreciation for the patterns of development rather than standards or precise predictions of what will happen at a given age. Culture, environment, health, temperament, and personality all affect the makeup of every child at every age. It is helpful that certain patterns have emerged and been documented, but they are never absolute."

We hope these developmental insights prove useful. Most of all, we hope that you will enjoy and learn as you and your students encounter the wonderful books Carol Otis Hurst and Rebecca Otis recommend.

Some Developmental Considerations

The Give and Take of Friendship

The early elementary years are a time of great social interest and learning. Upon entering kindergarten, the five year old takes one giant step away from family and moves more deeply into the world of peers. Making new friends looms large on the horizon. The next few years bring intense exploration of friendship and an increasingly complex understanding of what friendship means. The child feels both the pleasures and the pains, knows the give and the take. Within a few short years, friendship will become so central in the child's life that it will rival the importance of parents and teachers.

Bullies, Pests, and Teasing

While all children try out bullying, teasing and pesty behaviors at some point or another, these behaviors are especially prevalent at certain times in children's lives. A classroom filled with six year olds, for instance, will likely have some teasing, tattling and bullying. The six year old tends to be full of bravado, highly competitive, and into testing authority. The desire to be assertive and in charge is dominant. Using literature to explore ways of doing this without bullying or hurting others can be enormously helpful at this age. Around the time a child reaches seven, he/she enters a state of high self-awareness and sensitivity and the fear of being teased or bullied becomes great. Being teased or bullied can be especially painful to the child this age.

Isolation and Reaching Out Across Generations

At all ages, but especially in the early elementary years when children are still largely self-centered, it's important to show them they are capable of feeling empathy and reaching out to those in need. Young children are used to being the receivers of care; now they can begin to see themselves in the role of care-giver as well. This can be an enormously empowering feeling for a young child, to feel that they are capable of reaching out and making a difference in someone else's life.

Families

While peers are growing in importance for the child ages five through eight, family remains the center of the child's life. Children at these ages love reading about families in literature, exploring the wide range of similarities and differences. Through literature, children continue to broaden their vision of family, appreciating that not all families are the same in what they do or how they're made up.

Several of the stories in this section deal with issues of sibling rivalry. These stories can help children to see that they are not alone in their feelings about siblings. They can also help children learn some new ways of dealing with their feelings which will improve relations with their peers as well.

Working Together

Cooperation and negotiation are skills that do not come easily to the early elementary-age child, especially to the five and six year old who are still firmly placed at the center of their own universe and find it hard to see the world from any other point of view. At the same time, these children have a strong desire to work and play with peers and to be part of a larger community. Literature is a wonderful way to provide models of how people work together, giving children a chance to explore what it means to share and be fair at a time when they are not personally involved in the negotiation.

Thanks

We wish to thank the group of primary grade teachers who read sample sections of this book while still in draft form. Their candid criticisms and thoughtful words of encouragement were invaluable to us as we worked to make this book as useful to classroom teachers as possible.

Thank you:

Terry Kayne, first/second grade teacher in Greenfield, Massachusetts

Erin English, first grade teacher in Cincinnati, Ohio

Elisabeth Olivera, kindergarten teacher in Holyoke, Massachusetts

Cynthia Donnelly, first grade teacher in Springfield, Massachusetts

We also wish to thank *Nancy Ratner* for her careful editing, *Leslie and Jeff Woodward* for their pleasing design, and *Roxann Kriete* and *Mary Beth Forton* for their shepherding of this project.

Carol Otis Hurst and Rebecca Otis
April 1999

Introduction
Using Children's Literature:
A Cautionary Note

Books here
Books there
Books and poetry everywhere
Hundreds of books, thousands of books
Millions and billions and trillions of books

WE ARE STARTING OFF with a bit of hyperbole and a rather clumsy paraphrase of Wanda Gag but it makes our point that, to create literate students and to function as an effective learning community, every elementary classroom needs an ample supply of books. Kids need books to entertain, to educate, to explore, to excite and to soothe. Teachers need children's trade books to inspire, motivate, instruct and delight.

When books are shared in a classroom, the characters and stories become part of that learning community. Children retell the stories to themselves and to each other, incorporating the stories and characters into their play, their work and their conversations. In classrooms where trade books are read frequently, children develop favorite authors and illustrators. They recognize the work of those artists and choose their own books based on their previous experience. They read their favorite stories over and over and when they do so, they begin to learn the conventions of print, picking out familiar phrases and absorbing information about how words and language work.

We can use those trade books to start discussions, to pique children's interest in a subject to be explored, to answer some questions and to pose new ones. We identify with characters, recognizing others or ourselves in some of the feelings and reactions we get from reading the stories, and we get life lessons from the lives we glimpse in those stories.

However, when we use literature solely for the lessons the story teaches, we risk warping or distorting the book and missing its literary value. Since in this book we intend to explore ways in which children's literature can be used to spark discussions and activities related to interpersonal relationships, we want to remind the reader that it is easy to distort literature for educational purposes. We can find many books in which the stories consist entirely of thinly veiled lessons. The moral of the story is clear and the intent of the story is to relate that moral. These books are sometimes called "values literature" and reaching for one when such a lesson is in order is often tempting.

Such books, however, defeat our purposes in two ways. First, children seldom learn the intended lesson from such books. When we share, we do not do so because some parent or teacher read us a book in which two little elephant friends learned to share and lived happily ever after. We share because the people in our lives whom we respect shared and we saw them doing so as we grew older. We then found that when we shared with others, life became smoother and more pleasant. It is a rare child who models his or her behavior after a lesson from a book.

Second, such lesson books defeat us because they destroy other literature for children. When children recognize a book as a sermon (and they do so with alarming speed), they begin to suspect the intent of other books. They stop looking forward to shared books with delight and prepare instead for a sermon. This weakens the literary experience.

Publishers also fall victim to the lesson books. They produce what we ask for, and if we ask for books by value rather than by genre or author or illustrator, the publishers will too often give us those narrow lesson books.

With possible exceptions like Dr. Seuss and Leo Lionni, few authors can write fables or moralistic literature that children consistently respond to with delight. In general, if your first reaction on reading a kid's book is to say, "This book teaches that...," it is probably not a good book. We need books that are well written and illustrated with believable characters. We need books that have been written because the author had a story to tell, not because he or she had a lesson to teach. Choosing books to use with children for any purpose should start with those criteria in mind.

So, we want good books in our classrooms, but what qualities make a book good? The problem is that whenever we try to establish a standard for good literature, some author or illustrator creates a work that breaks some or all of those rules and produces something wonderful to surprise us. That surprise, in fact, is one of the elements of good literature. Good books do surprise us. If it is a story we have heard before in one form or another, the illustrations should startle or delight us with an interpretation that goes beyond the words. The words, whether they tell a story, describe an experience, or inform us in some other way, should be aptly chosen for their intended audience.

Perhaps the best way to judge a book for children is to see whether we, as living breathing adults, can be reached by it. If it is supposed to be sad, it should bring a lump to our throats. Although it is important to remember the audience for which the book is intended, if it doesn't speak to audiences beyond that intended age range, it will quite likely fail with any audience. There is no upper age limit for a good book.

There are many sources to aid in the selection of children's books and those are good places to start. However, even if the critics like a book, it does not mean that you will. Don't use a book you yourself don't like, no matter who says it is wonderful. If you don't like it, you won't present it well and your distance from it will be apparent. Choose books you like a lot to use with your children. Your joy will come through and carry the book to the listeners.

While we're cautioning about the use and misuse of children's books in the classroom, here's another note of caution. Since some very good stories deal with true to life experiences in a sensitive way, we sometimes attempt to use them to help children get through their own tragedies and traumas. A child's dog has died and we ache for that child's grief. In an effort to help, we reach for a book about a child whose dog has died and that is usually a mistake.

It would be wonderful if, before that child's beloved pet died, he or she had known characters who experienced grief and dealt with it realistically. (Lois Lowry, Newbery Award winning author, has said that reading *The Yearling* by Marjorie Rawlings when she was a child taught her how to grieve as an adult.) Weeks or months after the death of the pet, the child might be ready to hear a good story about death, but usually at the moment of trauma and for some time afterward the child does not need a book. That child needs us to open our arms and hearts to talk, to listen and to mourn. Any time we are using literature that deals with sensitive topics, we need to watch and listen to our children carefully. Books are powerful. They can open doors we did not mean to open and we need to be aware that true bibliotherapy is probably best done by a skilled counselor.

With all those caveats in mind, we have written this volume to suggest some very good books to read with kindergartners through second graders. We have also included some activities and discussion questions that may help children better understand and appreciate those books, and we have proposed some ways in which the stories can be extended to promote activities and discussions about interpersonal relationships. We hope you will look at them, not as lesson plans, but as suggestions for your own classroom communities.

In General: Book Discussions and Activities

In the following pages, we list several special books that can be used to spark activities and discussions about interpersonal relationships. These books are good stories, designed to interest and delight young children.

When we, as adults, read a good book, most of us like to talk to someone about it. If our friends have not yet read the book, we usually tell them just enough about it to get them to read it, too. We are delighted when we find others who have read the same book so we can talk to them about our feelings and reactions and listen to theirs. Sometimes these discussions are part of formal book discussion groups that are set up for that purpose, but more often the discussion is informal in nature and varies in length and substance.

It's important to give early readers that same opportunity to discuss books.

Finding Ways to Discuss a Story

Many of the activities we will suggest are designed to spark book discussion. If children are not accustomed to hearing adults talk about books, they will need lots of examples and role modeling to learn how to do it. Once they learn how, most children will just start talking without much prodding. They will finish a book and immediately look around for someone to talk to about it. When that stage is reached, you won't need many of the ideas for discussion that we have listed in this book.

There are also subjects raised within a story that can be used as stepping stones into discussions and activities about particular topics. These discussions are often where the real teaching and learning in a classroom can occur if an atmosphere is established where individuals know that their thoughts and ideas will be respected and their voices will be heard.

However, it's easy, as teachers, to fool ourselves into thinking that a question and answer session conducted by a teacher is a classroom discussion. We ask questions and one or two children give us the answers we are looking for. We discussed, right? Not quite. Good discussion is more of a dialogue than a question and answer period. It begins with engaging questions which do not have right or wrong answers, and it involves many people in conversation, although not all at the same time. Participants treat each other's opinions with respect and each person is given the opportunity to contribute.

These dialogues may well start with a question that the teacher has carefully constructed to bring out opinions, interpretations and divergent views. However, the teacher participates in such discussions by making meaning and forming opinions, just as every other member of the group does, rather than as the sole source of wisdom.

Sharing Illustrations in a Classroom

Sharing picture books prior to a discussion is always a question in logistics. Most picture books have a few lines of text with each page dominated by the pictures. If the teacher stands in the front of the room and reads the text, he or she then has a decision to make. If each picture is shared as the page is turned, the process of roaming the room showing that picture is so time-consuming that the story itself can be lost. On the other hand, in many books, those pictures are an intrinsic part of the story. Many teachers then adopt what we facetiously call the "teacher's swipe": a rapid swishing back and forth of the page in front of the class. Of course, no one has time to focus but we do get on with the story.

The best scenario is for the teacher to sit with the kids seated on the floor as close to her as possible. A teacher very familiar with the story can then show the necessary pictures with a minimum of fuss.

However, that will not provide enough time for most children to examine the pictures thoroughly, so the teacher will also want to allow time for ample viewing either before or after the book sharing. This simply involves making the book available so children can leaf through it at leisure in the classroom. After the book sharing, even more details can be extracted if the book is viewed by two children at a time, each with the specific assignment of pointing out details the other might have missed in the illustrations or the text.

Choosing Activities That Will Enhance Understanding

Activities emanating from a work of literature can lead to greater understanding but they can also be misused. The fact that you can do something related to the reading does not necessarily mean that you should. Even the fact that a given activity is lots of fun may not be reason enough to take class time to do it. For instance, making mobiles, puppets or dioramas are activities that could emanate from almost any story, but such activities may just distract us from our purpose. They may be fun but they are not necessarily worth our time and effort.

Also, activities based on literature should never distort or trivialize the work. They should make sense. Activities should extend the meaning of the book, help the child better understand it or prepare the child for better understanding of other reading yet to come. We all, teachers and children alike, need a sign on our desks asking, "Why am I doing this?"—and everyone in that classroom ought to know what the answer is.

The Give and Take
of Friendship

Chester's Way
by Kevin Henkes

Scholastic, 1988   ISBN 0 590 44017 9

Comments

Kevin Henkes reaches out to young children so effectively through his stories that we could write an entire book using his picture books alone. We have chosen this particular story because, although the characters in it are mice, most of us will recognize ourselves in their actions and reactions.

Henkes often creates vignettes involving mice characters which he places on the page surrounded by lots of white space. This has the effect of making the characters seem very small. However, he varies the size of these vignettes, stretching some across the page and always offering multiple views on a spread. Often his characters speak directly to us in cartoon-style speech in addition to speaking through the story line. The tails and ears of the characters reflect their feelings, as do their mouths and body language. It is important, therefore, when sharing this book, that children see the illustrations as they hear the story. It is available in a big book edition which can make that setup more feasible.

Summary

According to his mother and father, Chester has a mind of his own and his own way of doing things. Chester tells us about his ways at the beginning of the book. He likes order and unvarying routine. Safety conscious, he double-knots his shoes and uses hand-signals when he rides his bicycle. He lives by rigid rules.

His best friend Wilson is remarkably like Chester and the two are inseparable. They enjoy games together and Henkes gives us many examples of their pleasant pursuits. At Halloween they wear costumes which reflect their close relationship: salt and pepper shakers, two mittens, ham and eggs, two peas in a pod.

Then, Lilly moves into the neighborhood. She is as different from Chester and Wilson as we can imagine. She is exuberant, a leader, and a risk-taker. She wears a crown on her head to show that she is, as she shouts, the queen who likes everything! Even her ever-present cowboy boots are adorned with stars. She wears nifty disguises, carries a squirt gun and often talks backwards to herself as she walks along the street.

We are not surprised that Chester and Wilson are aghast at this loud child who flouts the rules. While they recognize that she too has a mind of her own, they refuse to play with her, rejecting all her overtures of friendship.

Then, one day, just as bullies are harassing Chester and Wilson while they ride their bikes, out of the bushes comes a large cat wearing cowboy boots with stars. The frightened bullies flee and Chester and Wilson acknowledge Lilly and thank her, albeit in a very formal and subdued manner.

That's the turn-around point. The careful twosome becomes a less cautious threesome. Lilly has some creative ideas which Chester and Wilson adopt. They also show her the advantages of some of their rules, such as the use of hand signals, which she adopts. Now, the Halloween costumes reflect their three-way friendship: the Three Blind Mice. All is well until Victor moves into the neighborhood.

Henkes does not tell us anything about Victor. We only see him as Chester, Wilson and Lilly view him on the last page. They are wearing Groucho Marx disguises and crouched behind a rock and Victor is leaping through the field chasing a butterfly with a determined look on his face.

After Reading the Story

Possible Questions and Topics for Discussion

- After sharing the book, ask children what they noticed about the story. Accept every answer and encourage them to enlarge upon their statements. Prod the discussion a bit with questions: Why do Chester and Wilson have so many good times together? How do you think Lilly feels when Chester and

Wilson avoid her? How do you think Chester and Wilson feel when they are avoiding Lilly? What else could Lilly have done to make friends?

- Encourage the children to speculate about what happens when two friends want to do things differently. Brainstorm all the possible solutions.

- Follow that brainstorming activity with a discussion about the advantages and disadvantages of having friends who are very different from ourselves. Is it possible to be too different? Have the children ever been scared by someone who is too different from them? Ask them what they can do about that.

Activities to Enhance Understanding

- Reread the book making lists of the things each character likes as you read. It may help to list these in a chart.

Chester Likes	Wilson Likes	Lilly Likes	Victor Likes
Croquet	Croquet	Everything	Chasing butterflies
Peanut butter sandwiches	Peanut butter sandwiches	Being queen	
		Wearing a cape	
Making his bed	Making his bed	Wearing cowboy boots	
Sandwiches cut diagonally	Sandwiches cut diagonally	Playing a drum	
Same side of the bed	Same side of the bed	Looking brave	
Double-knotting his shoes	Double-knotting his shoes	Talking backwards	
		Nifty disguises	
Toast with jam and peanut butter	Toast with jam and peanut butter	Waving at cars	
Carrying first aid kit	Carrying first aid kit	Carrying a squirt gun	
Playing baseball	Playing baseball	Popping wheelies	
Riding his bike	Riding his bike	Chasing butterflies	
Using hand signals	Using hand signals		

11

- Use the chart to make Venn diagrams to compare the characters:

- Use the chart to discuss aspects of the book: What does Lilly learn from Chester and Wilson and what do Chester and Wilson learn from Lilly? What do they learn to like about each other?

- Chester and Wilson are friends because they are so much alike. Later they become friends with Lilly even though she is quite different. Encourage children to draw pictures of themselves and a friend. They can tell the group about the ways they and their friends are alike and different.

- One of the skills in interpersonal relationships is recognizing feelings and moods in others. Look at each vignette in the book and use Post-its to note how each character is feeling. There are no right or wrong answers here. For instance, in the first picture, which shows Chester alone, introducing himself to us, his tail is down which could indicate sadness, but it has a curl in it. It could just be that he feels safe and comfortable. He has a slight smile on his face and his eyebrow is raised which could mean that he feels good about himself. Two pictures later, when he is shown getting out of bed, Chester looks quite happy. His arms are raised, his smile is broad, and his legs are kicking up a bit. This is a kid who is happy to greet the day.

- Part of being a friend is finding activities to do with others that they would enjoy. After reading the book, we know a lot about each of the characters and can begin to theorize about characteristics that have been implied but not directly men-tioned. Ask children to contribute to a list of activities they like to do and then speculate about how Chester, Wilson, and Lilly might react to each of them. For instance, how would the characters feel about doing the following:

Making sure their room is neat

Playing a game with lots of rules

Eating a new kind of food

Riding their bikes through an obstacle course

Riding their bikes through the woods

Playing in the mud

Seeing a scary movie

Meeting new kids

Leading the class in a song

Learning a folk dance

Dancing to rock music

- Provide small reproductions of each character and suggest that children place the character's picture beside activities they think that character would enjoy.

- We don't know much about Victor from this book but we assume that Chester and Wilson and certainly Lilly will want to learn more about him. Children may be willing to speculate on how Victor feels about moving into the new neighborhood. Have children use magic markers to draw simple happy and sad faces on a chart to predict some of Victor's feelings in different situations.

- Make a list of ways Chester, Wilson and Lilly could make Victor feel welcome. From that list design a series of activities to make newcomers to the classroom feel welcome. Decide together which things should be done on the first day, second day, etc. Some possibilities might include the following: assigning a guide or playmate to the newcomer; making gifts and cards or writing letters; putting up information sheets about each newcomer; having the newcomer lead a new game or activity.

- Do friends have to be alike? Have children fold a sheet of paper lengthwise. In one column have them draw pictures of the ways they and a friend are alike. In the other column have them draw ways in which they are different.

Frog and Toad Are Friends
by Arnold Lobel

HarperCollins, 1979 ISBN *0 06 444 0206*

Comments

Although the term "easy-to-read" is probably a misnomer since most research seems to show that short sentences with easy words are not easier for new readers than more natural text, Lobel was a master of the form. His books are full of warm, gentle humor and many children relate well to his characters.

His characters may be neurotic but they are lovable and his series of books about Toad and Frog have become classics. This volume won an Honor Newbery Book Award and was a finalist for the National Book Award. The format of the book invites comfort and accessibility.

Although this book concentrates on friendship and its ramifications, it also contains some possibilities for math and science activities. For instance, the story about the missing button provides an opportunity to conduct activities concerning properties and attributes—perhaps starting out with buttons. The story in which Frog makes Toad get out of bed in order to enjoy the spring together opens the door to activities about the calendar.

Summary

The cover of the book shows Toad reading to Frog. Toad is perched on a tree stump. Frog, on the ground close by his feet, has a thoughtful expression. His index finger is raised toward his mouth.

The title page shows Frog and Toad enjoying a cup of tea together. On the table of contents page, Toad is again reading to Frog. This time he sits on a toadstool while Frog is stretched out on the ground before him, chin in hand. The table of contents page reveals that there are five stories in this short, easy-to-read book.

The set-up in this book is unusual. The large-print text dominates the page with small illustrations. Lobel uses watercolors and a palette of greens and browns for his work. "Spring" is the first story and an excited Frog is shown rapping on Toad's front door. Remnants of snow lie on the roof and on the ground near the picket fence and mailbox. Frog is trying to tell Toad that spring has arrived but all we get from the "voice" inside the house is "Blah!" and later, "I am not here."

Frog walks right into Toad's darkened house, past a comfortable armchair with reading lamp and an unlit fireplace. Toad lies in bed with a nightcap on his head. Frog pushes and pulls Toad out into the spring sunshine where he is blinded by the light. Spring, apparently, is the beginning of the new year for these folks and Frog is looking forward to the activities the two friends can do together—skipping, running, swimming, and counting stars. But Toad is not tempted. All he wants to do is go back to bed, which he does directly, asking to be wakened in May— actually, half past May.

Frog is unwilling to wait until May for his friend. Going to Toad's calendar which still shows the month of November, Frog begins tearing off pages. Rushing back to Toad's slumber, Frog now informs him that it is May. Toad checks out the calendar and indeed it is May. Cheerfully Toad leaves his bed and the two friends investigate the spring.

"The Story" is the next chapter. This time it is Frog who is in bed looking, as Toad says, too green even for a frog. He's in Toad's bed and, in the illustration, Toad is giving him a cup of hot tea. Frog demands a story but Toad's creative powers are not cooperating. Thinking that walking up and down on the porch might get the muse working, Toad does so but to no avail.

Frog sits up in bed to see Toad standing on his head but even standing on it for a long time brings no good story ideas for Toad. Pouring water on his head is also unproductive. Next he bangs his head against a wall but that makes him feel terrible. Fortunately, Frog is feeling a bit better and can vacate the bed. Frog offers to tell Toad a story and then does so, telling him all that has happened in the story so far. That's enough for Toad. He's fast asleep.

"A Lost Button" has the two friends enjoying a long walk together through the woods and along the river. When they get back outside Toad's house, Toad realizes that he has lost one of the buttons on his jacket. Frog suggests that they retrace their walk to look for the button. Frog finds a button in the tall grass which Toad rejects, insisting that his button was white, not black like the one Frog has found. Nevertheless Toad deposits the black button in his pocket.

A sparrow finds the next button but it is a two-holed button rather than the four-holed one Toad is looking for. Putting that button in his pocket, Toad walks on with Frog who discovers another button on the dark path which Toad declares too small to be his missing button. He puts it in his pocket and they're off again.

The square button the raccoon brings is the wrong shape, as is the thin button Frog finds in the mud. This is too much for Toad. He loses his temper in frustration, runs into his house and slams the door. There on the floor of his house is the white, four-holed, big, round, thick button that belongs on his jacket. Toad is worried about all the trouble he has made for his friend Frog. He sews his found buttons all over his jacket and gives the jacket to Frog the next day, much to Frog's delight.

The next story shows Toad and Frog about to go swimming. Toad is going behind the rocks to change into his suit although Frog is not going to wear one. Toad is obviously worried about his bathing suit because he insists that Frog must not look at him until he gets into the water.

Once in the water, the two friends have a grand time. Frog is a fast swimmer and Toad swims more slowly but with fewer splashes. Then a turtle arrives. Toad is concerned. He asks Frog to tell the turtle to go away so that he won't see Toad's bathing suit. That news brings others to the river. Some lizards, a snake, two dragonflies and a field mouse want to see Toad in his funny looking suit and they take up a perch beside the river.

Toad resolves not to get out of the water until they leave. Frog pleads with the others to go away. Toad is getting cold. At last he stands beside the river clad in a shoulder to ankle bathing suit with broad green stripes. The animals love it. They all laugh. Frog laughs too. Toad asks him why he is laughing. "Because," says Frog, "you DO look funny in your bathing suit." Toad agrees and as we see him walk toward home wearing his funny bathing suit, his head is held high.

"The Letter" gives us a sad Toad sitting on his porch, chin in hands, as Frog approaches. According to Toad, he is always sad this time of day because it is mail time and Toad never gets any mail. The two friends sit and sadly look at Toad's empty mailbox together.

Frog hurries home and writes something on a piece of paper. He addresses an envelope, "A Letter for Toad." He gives the letter to a snail with the instructions to put it in Toad's mailbox. Snail agrees and sets off to do so. Frog rushes to Toad's house where Toad is taking a nap. Frog urges him to get up and wait for the mail. Toad refuses—there is no point; there will be no mail. Frog is getting worried. There is no snail and no letter in sight.

Now Toad is up and wondering why Frog keeps looking out of the window. Frog tells Toad that he has written him a letter. Toad wants to know what it says and Frog tells him what the letter says—that he is glad they are best friends. Toad is delighted. They sit and happily wait for the mail. Four days later, the letter-bearing snail arrives and Toad is very pleased.

After Reading the Story

Activities to Enhance Understanding

- Make a list of the ways Frog and Toad show they care about each other.

- Make a list of the activities Frog and Toad enjoy doing together.

- Have children make two lists like those above for activities that they and a good friend enjoy doing together.

- Look back at *Chester's Way* and compare Frog and Toad to Chester, Wilson and Lilly. Look at the list of activities on page 13. Which of those would Toad and Frog like to do?

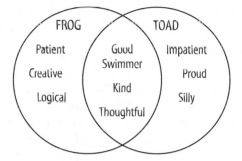

FROG — Patient, Creative, Logical

Good Swimmer, Kind, Thoughtful

TOAD — Impatient, Proud, Silly

- Frog and Toad are friends but they are not just alike. Use a Venn diagram such as the one above to show their shared and different qualities.

- Toad reads aloud to Frog. Apparently, he is the skilled reader although not the most sensible thinker. Pair off and have children try some reading aloud to each other.

- Although Toad and Frog have different personalities, they are good friends and appreciate each other's contributions. To demonstrate the fun of working together and the success of two contributors, try a technique called "Split Images" suggested in *Bringing It All Together* by Johnson and Lewis. In this activity two lines of children sit facing each other.

Children are told that they must not turn around and must talk only to the person facing them. A book is selected in which the illustrations are large and carry most of the story, since they will not be hearing the words. (*Tuesday* by David Wiesner works very well for this activity.) Encourage the children to tell their partners everything they see.

The book is shown to the group in this manner: the cover of the book is shown to the children facing one way; the title page is shown to children facing the other way. The first group sees the first page; the second group sees the next page and so on until the entire picture book is finished. As the children facing the book see the page, they should be talking rapidly to their partners, telling them what they see. Each page is shown slowly enough that all facing that way have a chance to see it but not so slowly that they have time to read the text. When the entire book has been shared in this way, each child will have seen every other page and will have listened to a description of the intervening pages.

The partners then go off to reconstruct the story together verbally. They can also select a moment from the story that they would like to illustrate on a large sheet of paper and do so, working cooperatively. When the illustrations are finished, hang them in sequence on a large wall. Missing events can be related, illustrated or written out in text. Children will most likely want to see the book in its entirety to fill in the pieces they missed and to enjoy the book as a whole.

Thematically Related Stories

- In one story Toad is very concerned about his funny-looking bathing suit, not wanting others, even Frog, to see him in it. The animals do laugh at him but notice what Toad does about that laughter. Check out other books in which there is ridicule or teasing (see page 48) for some other ideas about handling teasing. *Ira Sleeps Over* by Bernard Waber or *Chrysanthemum* by Kevin Henkes would be two fine choices.

- Read the other Frog and Toad books and enter more words in the Venn diagram as you learn more about Frog and Toad.

- Compare the friendship of Toad and Frog to that of George and Martha in the series of books titled *George and Martha* by James Marshall, published by Houghton Mifflin. George and Martha are two large, awkward hippos who are great friends. In spite of their ups and downs and peculiar situations, their friendship endures. The books contain stories in which the ridiculousness of the adventure is balanced by the hippos' dignity and the affection they share. Is Toad more like George than Martha? How about Frog?

- Make a Venn diagram for George and Martha. Compare it to the Venn diagram you made for Frog and Toad.

Rosie & Michael
by Judith Viorst
Illustrated by Lorna Tomei

Aladdin, 1974   ISBN 0 689 71272 3

Comments

The variations between hard reality and wild imaginative situations make this book funny and also give us an opportunity to discuss likely and unlikely situations. The fact that the friendship is between a boy and a girl is a nice touch since children sometimes refuse opposite sex friendships around first or second grade. Rosie and Michael play tricks on each other and call each other unflattering names that may cause some adults to wince a bit but children will approach those aspects as part of the delight and reality of such relationships.

Summary

There is no real story line in this book but the reader can use the limited anecdotal information to surmise many of the details about the antics of Rosie and Michael. The book, with its outsized black and white illustrations, is written with alternating testimonies to friendship, specifically to one particular friend for each of our narrators. Rosie and Michael have obviously been friends for a very long time. Their friendship has been tested and found solid.

As Rosie and Michael take turns giving brief accounts of their relationship, we learn a lot about both children, their sense of humor, their sense of fair play and their frank assessment of their own and each other's good and not-so-good qualities. Some of the situations arise from the exaggerated inventions of their creative minds but others are based solidly in the real world. They have played tricks on each other and have consoled and encouraged each other through life's many ups and downs.

The illustrations are black and white cartoon-style and slightly overcrowded. However, the large-headed figures and all their accouterments add to the comic nature of the book.

After Reading the Story

Possible Questions and Topics for Discussion

- At several places in the book, either Michael or Rosie talks about something that he or she feels is important about the friendship. Take each one of those statements and talk about why it would be important to some people and have children decide whether or not it would be important to them. For instance, Michael says that Rosie always remembered what his favorite nickname was at the time. Do children have nicknames they like or don't like? See page 34 for some other discussion questions about nicknames.

- Look at the tricks Rosie and Michael play on each other. Are any of them dangerous? What is the worst thing that could have happened? What is the most likely outcome? What are the boundaries with jokes and tricks? How does a person react when someone goes too far? What clues could children get that might tell them they've gone too far? What can they do about it if they have gone too far?

- Talk about friendships between boys and girls. What's good about them? What's hard about them?

- Ask children to talk about how they feel when they're teased and how they deal with teasing from other kids or grown-ups.

- Make a list of the things that Rosie likes about Michael. Make another list of the things Michael likes about Rosie. Compare the two lists. Is there one-to-one correspondence?

Activities to Enhance Understanding

- Rosie and Michael remember important facts about each other such as their reading tastes and the way they are currently spelling their names. Have children make a list of similar important facts they know about one of their friends.

- Have children write or draw five things that would be important for a friend to know about them.

- Make a table such as the one below about each incident mentioned in the story:

Event	Rosie's Reaction	Michael's Reaction
Michael sprayed Kool-Whip in Rosie's sneakers.	Rosie probably was surprised and not pleased.	Michael thought it was funny.
Rosie put a worm in Michael's sandwich.	Rosie ...	Michael ...
Michael covered a hole with leaves and told Rosie to jump on it.	Rosie ...	Michael ...

- To get some practice interpreting reactions to tricks, role play "What If I Did...?" Two children sit across from each other. One child asks the other a question such as, "How would you feel if I played a trick on you by taking all your pencils?" The other person responds non-verbally with hand-gestures or facial expressions. The first person interprets it: "You would not care." The second person affirms or negates that interpretation and then it's the other's turn to pose a question. After one round, switch to verbal responses, encouraging children to be as honest as possible.

- Further explore reactions to practical jokes or tricks with a graphing activity. Place the tricks listed in *Rosie & Michael* on a graph. Children place face stickers on the graph to show how they would react to such a joke, after first deciding

together what each of the faces means: funny, hurt, don't care
or angry. (See sample graphs below.)

If someone …	I'd feel …
sprayed Kool-Whip in my sneakers	
let the air out of my basketball just before a game	
dug a hole & covered it with leaves & told me to jump on it	
put a worm in my tuna salad sandwich	
called me a gorilla face	
called me a banana head	

Thematically Related Stories

- Read the book *Mud Flat April Fool* by James Stevenson. The
jokes fly fast in this adventure of the Mud Flat inhabitants. (See
page 89 for another book about the Mud Flat characters.)
George has a lapel rose that squirts and Newt has a dollar with
a string attached. Compare the pranks in this book with those
in *Rosie & Michael*. Ask children how they would react if the
trick were played on them.

Ira Says Goodbye
by Bernard Waber

Houghton, 1988   ISBN 0 395 48315 8

Comments

One of the hard parts of love and friendship is experiencing the loss that comes through death or other circumstances in which good friends have to part. Books can help children deal with that grief, particularly if they are read at a time when the child is not experiencing actual loss. In this book, no one dies, but loss produces grief nonetheless.

The people in *Ira Says Goodbye* have different ways of grieving and each one, even Ira, eventually accepts that difference. Ira experiences the stages of grief that many psychologists would say are typical and even necessary. Ira's mother's suggestion that, after saying goodbye to their dear friends, they all bake an angel food cake is only a step away from the funereal feast many cultures use to deal with mourning.

Another topic dealt with in this book is the idea of hiding one's true feelings. Ira's right out there with his grief over Reggie's departure. Reggie, on the other hand, takes a different approach. His father has prepared him for the move by describing the great and wonderful things that their new town holds in store. Reggie clings to those thoughts and puts them between himself and Ira to keep from facing his own grief. It is only when the move can no longer be denied that Reggie breaks down in tears.

Discussing such personal and sometimes traumatic matters as loss and grief can be difficult for children. Keep a careful eye on children during and after these activities so that children who are having difficulties can get consolation, comfort and even counseling if necessary.

Summary

This is a sequel to *Ira Sleeps Over* (see page 43). We know there's trouble from Ira's expression on the cover of the book. His mouth is open. He clutches the banister as he climbs the stairs (exactly the opposite of the cover of *Ira Sleeps Over*). Obviously saying goodbye is not all right with Ira.

On the title page Ira and Reggie are walking together. Their steps are long because Reggie is being pulled along by his dog who is chasing a butterfly.

As Ira talks to us from the first page, he looks sad. He leans against the porch railing, hands in his pockets. Reggie is moving away and Ira has learned about this from his sister. We know how she likes to tease from her actions in *Ira Sleeps Over*.

It's hard not to hate Ira's sister as she hangs by her knees from the tree near the porch railing, her expression gleeful as she tells Ira the news, bit by tantalizing bit. Ira tries to leave as she taunts him with pieces of information. Somebody is going to move in two weeks. At last we hear the dreadful news. Reggie is moving far away.

Ira is in denial but his parents confirm the news. They have just heard the news themselves and were coming to tell him. They supply the details—he is moving to Greendale, a six hour drive away.

On the next pages we see the wonderful things Reggie and Ira have shared—their tree house, a secret hiding place in the basement, the shows and the two-member club. The memories go on. They came to each other's birthday parties, shared their baseball card collection, took care of each other's pets. When Reggie broke his leg and was in the hospital, Ira sent him a home-made get well card, and when Ira visited his distant grandparents, Reggie sent him a "miss-you" card.

Even their turtles, Felix and Oscar, are best friends and share a turtle tank. Ira must now go to see Reggie and tell him how sorry he is. For a short time they grieve together but Reggie is transformed overnight. The next day he is overjoyed about the move. Reggie's father has told him about the wonders of

Greendale. There's a snorting killer shark in the aquarium there. Ira did not know that sharks snorted but Reggie assures him this is true. There's an amusement park in Greendale, a lake with swans and ducks yearning to be your friends. And the people in Greendale are so friendly they stop and say hello no matter how many times a day they see you.

Ira tries to remind Reggie that people here are friendly, too. "Some are even best friends," he says. But Reggie is still spouting on about Greendale. His Uncle Steve, a professional football player, lives in Greendale and Reggie will see him every day and learn how to be a great football player himself. The separation begins. Reggie takes back his half of the baseball card collection and Oscar, his pet turtle. Ira protests. Oscar and Felix are best friends. They cannot be separated. In an example of complete projection, Ira tells how the turtles will be so upset by the separation that they will die. Reggie will not be deterred. He takes Oscar, and Ira, in an act of selflessness, insists that he take Felix, too.

Ira has gone from denying that Reggie is moving to protesting and now he becomes angry. Reggie irritates him sometimes. He uses the same joke on the telephone over and over again. He laughs with his mouth open when he eats but, most of all, Reggie does not care about friendships. Ira cannot wait for

Reggie to leave. He sure hopes the next neighbor will be a better kid than Reggie.

The day comes. The movers start loading up Reggie's household items as Ira watches. Ira's back faces us. His shoulders are slumped, hands at his side. Reggie's family and Ira's family mingle together as they say their good-byes.

The parents and even Ira's sister are all hugging each other but the two boys just stand there. Reggie is holding the tank with Felix and Oscar inside. Suddenly, to Ira's amazement, Reggie begins to cry. He is inconsolable. When he finally stops crying, Reggie hands the turtle tank to Ira. Ira gives Reggie his half of the baseball cards. They all wave goodbye as they drive off. Reggie is smiling as he waves from the back of their car. Ira's mother brings her family back inside to bake an angel food cake.

That night, Reggie calls Ira with the same tired joke, but Ira does not protest. Reggie invites Ira to spend the next weekend at his new house in Greendale. The mothers talk and make arrangements. Ira rushes up the stairs to pack in an illustration that looks like the one on the cover, but subtle differences make it a joyful rather than a mournful scene. The last picture is the same as the one on the cover. Only the text is different but we give that picture a whole different interpretation because of it.

After Reading the Book

Possible Questions and Topics for Discussion

- After sharing the story, go back through it page by page to elicit information on how Ira feels throughout the story.

- Both Reggie's family and Ira's family help their children deal with the coming loss. Find the ways in which that happens.

- Most children have either moved themselves or have had friends or family who have moved away. Encourage them to tell what the good and bad parts of their own moves have been.

- Why do people move? Reggie's family is moving because of his father's new job. The family will also be living closer to some of their relatives—Reggie's uncle, for instance. List some other reasons for moving.

- Ask children what three things they would want to take along with them if they were moving. What three things would they want to leave behind with a friend?

- How can children let someone know they are feeling sad or that they will miss them if it's necessary to say goodbye? Make a list of some words that can be used to express sorrow.

- The turtles in this story are named Felix and Oscar. Kids who watch re-runs on television may be able to tell the others about "The Odd Couple" from which these names were taken.

Activities to Enhance Understanding

- Reggie and Ira plan to keep in touch by phone and through visits. Letters and the Internet are other ways in which distant friends can communicate. Suggest that each class member communicate with a distant friend or relative in some way over the next few days and then tell the class about it. Make a list of advantages and disadvantages for each method of keeping in touch.

- If the class has had someone move away, find a way to get in touch. Write letters or make a speaker phone call.

- Help someone who is about to move away by having children learn about the new community. Make that child the focus of all sorts of activities for saying goodbye. Interview the child. Find out what the child expects to miss, what the child is looking forward to, how the child plans to keep in touch and how he or she plans to make new friends.

Thematically Related Stories

- Read some of the other good books about moving. Judith Viorst's *Alexander, Who's Not (Do You Hear Me? I Mean It!) Going to Move* has Alexander caught up in angry denial at the thought of moving. In Marjorie Sharmat's *Gila Monsters Meet You at the Airport,* the narrator has many fears about a new home. Angela Johnson's *The Leaving Morning* is a sensitive book about saying goodbye to friends and to an apartment full of memories. Frank Asch's bear hero of *Goodbye House* becomes very human as he says goodbye to the home he has cherished.

A Toad for Tuesday
by Russell Erickson

Beechtree, 1998   ISBN 0 688 16325 4

Comments

Most of the books we have cited are picture books. You can't really call this one a chapter book either, since it's all one chapter. Let's call it a short, illustrated novel which makes a good read-aloud choice for young children. It deals with making and keeping friends, sharing, telling stories, explaining one's behavior and reaching out to others. Many young children have trouble retaining a long story, especially one with few pictures, so be sure that you stop often and get recaps and predictions from the listeners while reading this story.

Summary

Warton and Morton are brother toads who share a household. Things work out well for them in spite of the fact that they are very different in living habits and in character. They divide up their chores according to their likes and dislikes: Warton does the cleaning and Morton cooks. It's Morton's fine cooking of beetle brittle that inspires Warton to leave their warm home in the middle of winter to bring some of it to their old Aunt Toolia, thus setting the adventure in motion.

Morton protests mightily against Warton's plan. No toad should go out in the winter; Warton will freeze and be unable to get through the deep snow. He'll be alone and friendless up there.

Warton, however, devises a plan to overcome those obstacles. He will dress warmly and travel on skis. The fact that he has no skis and, indeed, has never skied before does not daunt him. Warton works for three days to make the skis. He dresses warmly, packs enough lunches to last for three or four days, an extra pair of mittens, a pair of slippers, and the beetle brittle and sets off. He has a bit of trouble figuring out how to use the skis but soon he's doing quite well.

When Warton stops for lunch, he rescues a deer-mouse from his upside down state in a snow bank. He shares his hot tea with the mouse, and the deer-mouse warns him against traveling through the wooded valley as Warton has planned to do. There is, apparently, a large and very nasty owl who patrols that area, breaking all custom by going about in the daytime. When Warton insists on going that way, the mouse gives him a red scarf to wear. It will, he says, inform any of the mouse's relatives that Warton is his friend.

Warton is almost through the wooded valley when the owl catches him. Warton crashes into a stone wall, injuring his foot. The owl takes him to his hollow tree and informs Warton that he will keep him until Tuesday, which is the owl's birthday. He intends, at that time, to have a toad birthday feast.

The owl insists on calling Warton "Warty" although the toad protests. Warton is told that he can do as he likes until Tuesday although his choices are not extensive. The owl's home is high in the tree, and with his hurt foot, there is little chance that Warton can escape.

The owl's home is a mess and Warton cannot resist cleaning and straightening. Even that first night, Warton lights some candles to make the home less dreary. As he does so, Warton begins to hum and the owl is nonplussed. Warton asks the owl for his name and when the owl confesses that he has none, Warton asks, "What do your friends call you?" But the owl has no friends. Warton names him George.

Warton makes tea, puts on his bathrobe and slippers and insists that George join him for a nighttime cup. Soon a reluctant owl is drinking tea with his projected dinner and telling about the joy of flying. He also confesses that he hunts in the daytime because he is unable to stay awake all night no matter how hard he tries.

Each day the owl is gone when Warton wakes up and Warton sees that another day on the calendar has been marked off. (The following Tuesday is circled.) Warton cleans the house and each day George comes back earlier and earlier. They share their nightly tea and exchange stories and information about themselves. George, however, reminds Warton frequently that he has not changed his mind about eating him on Tuesday.

Warton devises a plan to escape. He unravels his sweaters and builds a yarn ladder so he can get out of the tree. Time is of the essence and George keeps coming home earlier each day. Warton tells him, one night, about his favorite kind of tea, juniper berry. The berries are rare and he's only had it once but it was wonderful, Warton says.

Warton tests his yarn ladder on Sunday even though it's far from finished. It does appear to hold him, however, and he resolves to work even harder to finish it. He does hope that George will change his mind about eating him and that the ladder will be unnecessary. That day, however, George returns late and in a bad mood. He had gotten stuck in a log because of a very persistent fox. George eats some of Warton's beetle brittle and, as he replaces the box in Warton's pack, he spies the yarn ladder. George throws it out the door, destroying Warton's only hope of escape.

The next day is George's birthday. Warton is despondent until he hears a sound from inside the tree. Soon a mouse's head peeks through the floor. A whole troop of deer-mice have come to rescue Warton. They had seen him wearing the scarf and had seen him captured by the owl. Packing quickly, Warton does not notice that he has also packed a scrap of paper that was on the table. At the foot of the tree the mice are waiting, all fitted out with skis. They've made a pair for Warton as well and soon they set off in two long lines. Other creatures stare in astonishment as they go whizzing by. The skiers begin to sing a marching song and they go even faster.

Stopping to rest beside a frozen stream, Warton sees George locked in a death struggle with the fox. Warton dashes to help and the mice, after expressing their surprise that Warton would want to help his enemy, join in. As the fox sees the tiny horde dashing toward him on skis, he decides running is his best choice and he releases the owl. Badly beaten, George is still nevertheless surprised to hear that Warton is escaping. "Why?" he asks. Did Warton not see his note? The note had said that George was bringing home a surprise. He had intended that surprise to be a fish and some juniper berries for tea.

The owl says that he had fully intended to eat Warton until the night before when they had not spoken much. George had had time to think and had decided that having a friend was better than having a meal. George promises never to eat another toad or another mouse. Warton says goodbye to all his new friends and heads off to Aunt Toolia's.

After Reading the Book

Possible Questions and Topics for Discussion

- One way in which George and Warton become friends is through explaining their behavior to each other. Reread the points at which this is done and talk about what would have happened if each had explained his actions earlier.

- Find examples in the story of good manners. From there, begin a discussion about why and when good manners are helpful. Spend a day where manners are noticed and even exaggerated. Does it change the atmosphere in the classroom? At home?

- The owl calls Warton "Warty" even though Warton objects. Find out which children in the classroom have nicknames and how they feel about those nicknames. Are there children in the classroom who don't have nicknames but would like one? Do children think they can get a desired nickname to stick?

- There are three friendships in *A Toad for Tuesday:* one between brothers, one between very unlike creatures, and one with the large group of mice. Discuss the ways in which each of these friendships was made and some of the ways in which the friendships can be continued.

Activities to Enhance Understanding

- Upon completion of the story, make a list together of main events. Place those events on squares of colored paper and involve the children in placing them in order to make a flow chart. After displaying the flow-chart, ask children to decide what each character was feeling at that point in the story.

- Make a list of events in the story that turned out well in the end along with their outcomes.

- Warton and Morton's division of household chores makes good sense for them. Have children make a list of their own qualities and preferences that might be considerations in finding the jobs they would do best and like most.

- When Warton and George have their evening tea, a friendship develops through that sharing and the sharing of stories. Have a classroom tea party in which people pair off to share tea and stories. Make sure good manners prevail and that each is prepared with an amusing or interesting anecdote to tell.

Thematically Related Stories

- While discussing names, read the picture book *Chrysanthemum* by Kevin Henkes. In it a little girl is teased quite viciously at school, particularly by one child, because of her name. This story presents a chance to talk about the line between teasing and ridicule and a chance to talk about unusual and interesting names.

The Give and Take of Friendship

Selected Bibliography

Asch, Frank. *Goodbye House*. Simon & Schuster, 1986. ISBN 0 671 67927 9.

Erickson, Russell. *A Toad for Tuesday*. Beechtree, 1998. ISBN 0 688 16325 4.

Henkes, Kevin. *Chester's Way*. Scholastic, 1988. ISBN 0 590 44017 9.

-----. *Chrysanthemum*. Mulberry, 1996. ISBN 0 688 14732 1.

-----. *Julius, the Baby of the World*. Greenwillow, 1990. ISBN 0 688 08944 5.

Johnson, Angela. *The Leaving Morning*. Orchard, 1992. ISBN 0 531 08592 9.

Johnson and Lewis. *Bringing It All Together*. Heinemann, 1990. ISBN 0 435 08502 6.

Lobel, Arnold. *Frog and Toad Are Friends*. HarperCollins, 1979. ISBN 0 06 444 0206.

Marshall, James. *George and Martha*. Houghton Mifflin, 1973. ISBN 0 395 16619 5.

-----. *George and Martha: The Complete Stories of Two Best Friends*. Houghton Mifflin, 1997. ISBN 0 395 85158 0.

Sharmat, Marjorie. *Gila Monsters Meet You at the Airport*. Aladdin, 1980. ISBN 0 689 71383 5.

Stevenson, James. *Mud Flat April Fool*. Greenwillow, 1998. ISBN 0 688 15164 7.

Viorst, Judith. *Alexander, Who's Not (Do You Hear Me? I Mean It!) Going to Move*. Atheneum, 1995. ISBN 0 689 31958 4.

-----. *I'll Fix Anthony*. Aladdin, 1969. ISBN 0 689 70761 4.

-----. *Rosie & Michael*. Aladdin, 1974. ISBN 0 689 71272 3.

Waber, Bernard. *Ira Says Goodbye*. Houghton, 1988. ISBN 0 395 48315 8.

Wiesner, David. *Tuesday*. Clarion Books, 1991. ISBN 0 395 55113 7.

Bullies, Pests, and Teasing

Bootsie Barker Bites

by Barbara Bottner
Illustrated by Peggy Rathmann

Paperstar, 1992   ISBN 0 698 11427 2

Comments

Most of us can identify with the little girl in this story. She's stuck with Bootsie through no fault of her own. She and the bully are thrust together for the sake of their parents' comfort. The girls have nothing in common. Our narrator is interested in turtles and salamanders and she reads a lot. Bootsie thrives on domination. We are told that she bites although we never see her do so. In fact, although violence is feared, we see no violence and we suspect that there is none.

This is a story about intimidation. When the adults refuse to help with the problem, our narrator uses information she has gained from her reading to intimidate the person who is intimidating her. Although some adults will wish that Bootsie somehow will repent or reform during the story, most children will understand that the book is too short for such a solution.

Summary

We don't doubt that Bootsie bites although she does not do so in this book. We see her on the cover—dressed to go visiting in a lovely dress with sash and matching purse. The hat is large and black but the pink ribbon rescues it from what might have been a more menacing look. True, the cowboy boots are a bit intimidating but they are pink and match the dress. It's her teeth! Bootsie shows them all as she stares directly at us from the cover, and even though the corners of her mouth turn up, we know that's not a smile.

The title page shows Bootsie and a woman we later learn is her mother on the front doorstep of a dwelling. Their backs are toward us. Bootsie's mother is dressed all in lime green. (This is a family that believes in matching accessories.) She is carrying two packages. We later find out those are strawberries and a cake. From the lower left corner of the window, we see a rather frightened face peering out. Somehow we get the sense that, for one person at least, Bootsie and her mother are not welcome guests.

On the dedication page, the same child is hiding behind the drapes. Our narrator then explains that Bootsie's mother and hers are best friends. Our narrator is a slight little girl with her hair in neat braids. We get some sense of her age by the pull-toy turtle she has with her.

Things go well at first. She and Bootsie have a tea party with the strawberries and cake that Bootsie's mother has brought. Disaster does not strike until they play in the little girl's bedroom away from the adults. Pages fly as she tries to interest Bootsie in a book about turtles. Bootsie's mouth is open wide and we know she is yelling because her hostess is fleeing with her hands over her ears. She is terrified when Bootsie announces that she is a turtle eating dinosaur and the little girl is a turtle. The shadows on the wall take on the girls' assumed roles. At last Bootsie and her mother depart, but as they do so, Mrs. Barker announces that they will be back the next day.

The unhappy child tells her mother that she does not like playing with Bootsie but her mother says she has to learn to get along with all sorts of people. We see Bootsie kicking at a dog on the way home and sticking her tongue out at a baby in a grocery cart. The next day's visit is another disaster for our friend although Bootsie has a wonderful time pretending to be various kinds of terrifying dinosaurs, all of which are ready to eat our narrator.

At breakfast the next morning, our narrator spills her juice when she hears her mother say that Bootsie is staying overnight this time. She imagines her family being rushed off to the hospital as Bootsie waves goodbye from their doorway. The child panics and reveals her fears to her mother. Her mother thinks that all she has to do is tell Bootsie she does not want to play dinosaur this time. Our narrator knows better and so do we. Bootsie is not to be deterred by a mere statement of preference.

Bootsie arrives but this time our narrator is prepared. With camping equipment and a few tools spread out, she announces that she is a paleontologist and that she hunts dinosaur bones. Bootsie runs away in terror. Her parents are just leaving and Bootsie insists on going with them.

Before Reading the Book

Discussion Questions Prior to Reading

• This is a book that we can talk about step by step. Before reading the book, speculate together about the cover of the book. What do we know about Bootsie already? Looking at the first picture of the girls in the bedroom, we can learn a bit about Bootsie's hostess. What does she like to do? What is she interested in? This is also our first glimpse of Bootsie's destructive nature as she tears the book. Even the toys appear to be shocked at Bootsie's behavior.

While Reading the Book

Discussion Questions While Reading

• What are the little girl's alternatives at each particular point in the story? Make a list of them and discuss the possible results of each action as you read. For instance, she could try to fight Bootsie. The results don't look promising because Bootsie seems to be bigger and our narrator does not look like much of a fighter. She could tell the parents. (We later find out that she tries telling her mother about it—twice.)

After Reading the Book

Possible Questions and Topics for Discussion

• Speculate about some of the reasons why Bootsie behaves this way. It might be that she's not used to playing with other kids and does not know how, for instance. She might think our hostess is just pretending to be frightened. Kids might be willing to talk about how it is sometimes fun to scare or intimidate people and about how they feel when people scare or intimidate them.

- Our narrator tries several times to make playing with Bootsie a better experience. She tries to interest her in her books and her pet salamander. She tells her mother that things are not going well. What else might she try? She also tries imagining dreadful fates for Bootsie but that only soothes her temporarily. Her solution is to scare Bootsie or bully the bully. Make a list of things to do when confronted by a bully. Then speculate together about several possible outcomes of each action.

- Most of us, if we are honest with ourselves, will admit that we have bullied someone in our lives. This may be a good place for teachers to tell their stories of bullying and being bullied.

- Make a series of statements together that begin with "You know you're being a bully when..."

Thematically Related Stories

- Share *A Weekend with Wendell* by Kevin Henkes, another good book about bullies with a very different solution. Wendell is a bit less intimidating than Bootsie. In fact, he'd probably be described as bossy rather than as a bully. However, Sophie, his hostess for the weekend, finds him quite intimidating. Wendell insists on a dominant role when he visits Sophie. They play hospital and Wendell is the doctor. They play bakery shop and Sophie has to be the sweet roll. Wendell makes the rules, and for most of the book, Sophie just wishes for the weekend to be over. Sophie's mother and father share her consternation at Wendell's behavior and they, too, long for his visit to come to an end.

  Then, after Wendell has coated himself with shaving cream, Sophie squirts him with the hose as she plays fire chief and very soon the two are just having fun with no one being boss. When the weekend comes to an end, only Sophie's parents are relieved. After all, he did make quite a mess. Compare Sophie's solution with that of the narrator in *Bootsie Barker Bites*. Was Sophie's solution on your list of possible ways to handle a bully?

Ira Sleeps Over
by Bernard Waber

Houghton, 1979   ISBN 0 395 20503 4

Comments

The illustrations in this book are far from pretty. Their slapdash look can fool you into thinking they are carelessly done but a closer look reveals how sensitively Waber has shown the child's point of view. Ira's feelings are apparent in body language and facial expressions throughout the story. The story deals with teasing and the fear of being teased. The moral is clear but unstated. Most people fear being teased and much of the time those fears are unfounded.

Summary

Our first view of Ira is a sleepy one. On the cover he is wrapped in some sort of blanket and slippers. Sleepy-eyed, he clutches a worried looking teddy bear in his left hand, and one would think he is heading for bed, but he is descending the stairs. The title page shows a packed suitcase with the teddy bear seated in front of it.

Ira speaks directly to us. With outstretched hands and a wide smile he tells us that he is going to sleep overnight at Reggie's house, his first such adventure. The problem rears up immediately, however, on the next page as we get our first look at Ira's know-it-all sister. She leans out the window to taunt Ira as he sits on a railing outside the house and poses the question that will dominate the book, "Are you taking your teddy bear along?"

Ira's first response is negative. Of course he won't be taking his teddy bear to Reggie's house. The whole concept is ridiculous. But the taunter will not stop. She reminds Ira that he has never slept without his teddy bear before. The tone in her voice is audible to the reader.

A cat on the railing listens to Ira's reply. Ira will not mind not sleeping with his bear. His sister walks off carrying the cat. The seed is planted. Her deed is done. The next spread shows four vignettes of Ira as he goes about the house worrying, with the last vignette showing him back in his bedroom where the teddy bear waits on his bed.

His parents are good ones. They reassure him when he worries that Reggie will laugh at him for sleeping with his teddy bear. We learn a bit about Ira's family in these pictures. The father plays the cello or bass. His mother reads the newspaper. There's a picture on the wall of a ballerina and we suspect that it may be his mother in her younger days. The family apparently likes pets. They have a goldfish, a cat and a canary. His sister plays the piano, and just as Ira is feeling reassured about taking his teddy bear to Ira's house, she gets in another jab. "He'll laugh." Ira reconsiders his decision.

That afternoon the boys are together near Ira's house. We get the first perspective on the row house where Ira lives. Reggie has big plans for their sleep over. They are going to have a great time. Ira dares to raise the dreaded topic, "What do you think of teddy bears?" But Reggie is too engrossed in their plans for the evening. After a series of wonderful games and activities they will get to the best part—telling ghost stories. Ira's next question

shows his growing concern. "Does your house get very dark?" Reassured that it does, Ira asks again, "What do you think of teddy bears?" But Reggie rushes off without answering. Ira decides to take his teddy bear.

In the kitchen, his father and mother are cooking and they are happy with Ira's decision, but you-know-who, setting the table, takes a new tack. What about his teddy bear's babyish name of Tah Tah? Ira reverses himself. He will not take the teddy bear.

The fated hour arrives. Holding his suitcase, Ira stands by his front door getting a goodbye kiss from his mother. His sister, still at the dining room table, calls out, "Sleep tight," but somehow we know that her tone is not reassuring. Ira climbs over the porch railing to Reggie's house where Reggie stands in his doorway. This is the first time that we learn that the two boys actually live in adjacent houses.

The evening at Reggie's house proceeds just as Reggie has planned it. They go through all Reggie's junk treasures, try on some nifty disguises and play with the stamps from Reggie's father's office. The play gets rougher. They have a wrestling match and a pillow fight at which point Reggie's father declares it a night. The boys get into bed. Ira is to sleep in a cot by Reggie's bedside. Reggie starts his ghost story and apparently scares himself because he asks, "Are you scared?" Ira says he's not scared but Reggie needs to get something out of a drawer before he can go on. In the dim light Ira can just make out the shape of a teddy bear.

Reggie gets back into bed prepared to go on with his grizzly tale but Ira needs to know about that teddy bear. Is it Reggie's? Does he sleep with him all the time? Does the teddy bear have a name? Each question is met first with a pretense of not hearing the question but eventually Ira gets the picture. Reggie sleeps with his teddy bear every night and his teddy bear's name is Foo Foo. We also learn that Reggie has been afraid that Ira would laugh at him. Ira's on the way out of bed.

He's back at his house and his surprised family greets him at the door. Ira marches past them and up the stairs. Here's the cover picture on the next page. Ira heads back down the stairs with Tah Tah. His sister is not to be stifled. She says, "Reggie will laugh. You'll see how he'll laugh. He's just going to fall down laughing." But Ira knows better. "He won't laugh."

Back in Reggie's bedroom Ira is prepared to show his teddy bear and proclaim its name to Reggie but Reggie is sound asleep, clutching Foo Foo. There's no one to say goodnight to now but Tah Tah, and Ira does so as he settles down to sleep.

After Reading the Book

Possible Questions and Topics for Discussion

- Count the number of times Ira changes his mind in the story and identify the reason for each change. List and discuss those changes and their reasons.

- Most kids have been the victims of teasing and some may be willing to tell about someone who frequently teases them. Some of that teasing may well be done in a loving manner while other teasing, such as that of Ira's sister, is more likely to be mean-spirited. Help kids determine which kind of teasing they get. What resources do children have to help them when they are being teased or ridiculed?

- Some teasing seems to show a lack of respect for the person being teased. We are apt to give that teasing the name of "ridicule." Define respect. Children might be helped by a discussion of the line between respect and disrespect.

- Most kids will also admit that they sometimes tease others. A discussion can help them discover ways to know when they have gone too far and the other person is no longer having fun. It may be possible to come up with a word that anyone can say at any time to stop teasing or ridiculing behavior.

Activities to Enhance Understanding

- Make a list of facts you know about Ira's family from the story. After each item on the list have children place their names next to traits or habits which apply to their own family.

- There is an obvious opportunity here to show and share each others' treasured stuffed animals, especially teddy bears. Most of these have their own stories and kids should be encouraged to tell where their toys came from and what adventures they have had. Write each stuffed animal's story and display the stories.

- Give each child a cardboard circle on one side of which is printed the word "Teasing." Watch a taped TV sitcom together in which characters are teased. When children think there is teasing going on, have them hold up their signs. At each point, the tape should be stopped and the person or persons holding up their signs should explain. Continue the tape for a short sequence and then stop it again to discuss how the TV character is taking the teasing and what his or her alternatives were. Would that teasing be funny in real life?

Thematically Related Stories

- Read the book *The Million Dollar Bear* by William Kotzwinkle, illustrated by David Catrow. It concerns a bear that is treasured for its monetary value. A comparison of Ira and Reggie's bears with the ones in this story can lead to a good discussion about values.

- In *Chrysanthemum* by Kevin Henkes, a little girl is made miserable at school because others, particularly Victoria, ridicule her about her name. Read that story together and decide whether Chrysanthemum or Ira gets a better deal as far as teasing is concerned. Also compare the ways in which each character handles that teasing. Chrysanthemum wants to quit school and is crushed each time Victoria starts to tease. Although her parents are supportive, it is the teacher, Mrs. Twinkle, who helps Chrysanthemum when she reveals that her own first name is Delphinium. It is successful because all the children, including Victoria, like Mrs. Twinkle a lot. Ira, of course, needs no outside force. He rescues himself.

Bullies, Pests, and Teasing

Selected Bibliography

Bottner, Barbara. *Bootsie Barker Bites*. Paperstar, 1992. ISBN 0 698 11427 2.

Henkes, Kevin. *A Weekend with Wendell*. Mulberry, 1986. ISBN 0 688 14024 6.

-----. *Chrysanthemum*. Mulberry, 1991. ISBN 0 688 14732 1.

Kotzwinkle, William. *The Million Dollar Bear*. Knopf, 1995. ISBN 0 679 85295 6.

Waber, Bernard. *Ira Sleeps Over*. Houghton, 1979. ISBN 0 395 20503 4.

Isolation and Reaching Out
Across Generations

The Mitten Tree
by Candace Christiansen
Illustrated by Elaine Greenstein

Fulcrum, 1997   ISBN 1 55591 349 0

Comments

The wordless communication between the children and the old woman in this book becomes a game in which the woman knits mittens and hangs them on her tree and the children find and wear them. Later, they repay her with baskets of yarn with which to knit more mittens. Of course, each knows what the other is doing but they choose to keep the communication subtle. To acknowledge each other would ruin the game. Although the accent in this book is on that joyful relationship, the fact that at least one of those children is probably poor should not be missed. It isn't that he needs matching mittens, but rather that he has none.

Summary

A lonely old woman reaches out to a group of children in this book. We first see Sarah as a young woman, however, on the dedication page of the book. She appears in a framed photograph holding a child by each hand. The children carry lunch boxes and look ready for school. Her tiny house is seen in the background.

The first page describes how she used to walk her children to the blue spruce tree where they waited for the school bus. Now Sarah watches through the upstairs window of her neatly kept house as other children wait for the bus. She walks past those children every morning on her way to the mailbox wishing they would smile or wave but they do not. They seem not even to notice her.

One morning Sarah notices one little boy who stands apart from the other children who are making a snowman there at the bus stop. Dressed all in blue, he stands with his hands in his pockets, and when he climbs onto the school bus, Sarah notices that he has no mittens.

Returning to her warm and comfortable house, Sarah begins knitting blue mittens for the boy. Before the children arrive the next morning, Sarah has already hung the blue mittens from the old blue spruce tree. From behind a hedge Sarah watches the boy in blue as he spies the mittens. Quickly he puts them on and makes a big snowball which he throws high into the sky in celebration.

Sarah next notices that a little girl has mismatched mittens. Since her coat is red, Sarah knits red mittens for her and hangs them on the tree. Now Sarah looks carefully at the children as she goes to the mailbox, looking for children without mittens, and each day the children eagerly search the tree looking for the new treasures. Once or twice, Sarah thinks that the first little boy has seen her but he always looks quickly away.

We next see Sarah dozing in her chair by the fire. A large cat sleeps on the rug by her feet near five pairs of mittens which are ready to be hung on the tree. We are told that, although the children and Sarah have never spoken to each other, Sarah feels like they are family.

On the last day before winter vacation, Sarah has outdone herself. She's knitted mittens with every bit of yarn and the tree, when the children arrive, is resplendent with colorful mittens. Still no one looks at Sarah as she heads back into her house.

On the porch of her house a surprise waits for Sarah. A lovely basket decorated with a white bow bears balls and balls of colorful yarn. We are told that the custom continues: Sarah knits and new yarn appears. Supposedly Sarah does not know the source of the yarn and the children do not know the source of the mittens, but the person whose feet and arms we see putting down a new basket of yarn is dressed all in blue.

After Reading the Story

Possible Questions and Topics for Discussion

• How is Sarah unlike Mr. Hatch in *Somebody Loves You, Mr. Hatch* (see page 55)? Are there ways in which they are alike?

• Look for details that tell you about Sarah's real family.

• Look for signs that show that Sarah cares a lot about the place where she lives.

• Notice how the patterns on the mittens become more complicated.

Activities to Enhance Understanding

• Find someone who can teach the children how to knit or weave simple items like a warm scarf or hat. Make a collection of warm clothes like scarves and mittens. Have children leave them as anonymous gifts where they think they will do the most good.

• Find out what kinds of needs there are in your community. Is there something the children can do to help?

• Have children identify one person in their school to whom they have never spoken. How would they know if that person were lonely? What would happen if they smiled at him or her? Have them try it. Discuss what happens over a period of time.

- Do children have a family member who does not live with them who might be lonely? What could they do about that?

Thematically Related Stories

- There's a parallel between this book and *Mr. Nick's Knitting* by Margaret Wild and Dee Huxley. Mr. Nick and Mrs. Jolley both ride the train to work and knit as they travel. Mr. Nick knits sweaters while Mrs. Jolley knits toy animals. When Mrs. Jolley becomes ill, Mr. Nick visits her in the hospital and then proceeds to knit her a quilt of their shared memories. After reading both books, children might be able to think of items they can make to give to friends.

Somebody Loves You, Mr. Hatch
by Eileen Spinelli
Illustrated by Paul Yalowitz

Simon & Schuster 1992   ISBN 0 027 86015 9

Comments

Because this book deals with the effects an unexpected anonymous gift has on its lonely recipient, it provides an opportunity to discuss anonymous giving. Isolation and the results of reaching out to others are also main themes in the book. It may help students take a second look at people in their midst who are lonely and isolated.

Summary

This is a sweetly sentimental story that works. It has ties to Valentine's Day but it's much more than that. In it, we make the acquaintance of Mr. Hatch, who is a loner at the beginning of the story. He works in a shoelace factory where he eats a solitary and Spartan lunch. His daily routine is unvaried, and people, when they speak of him at all, remark that he "keeps to himself."

Then, one day (he hasn't noticed it is Valentine's Day), the postman, with whom Mr. Hatch has never spoken, delivers a package and the two men speak briefly. The package contains a heart-shaped box of candy and an unsigned note stating, "Somebody loves you." Puzzled, Mr. Hatch goes about his daily chores but the message keeps repeating in his head and eventually he laughs out loud at the thought. The laughter soon leads to dancing and, of course, eating the candy.

Mr. Hatch changes to a more colorful outfit, even adds a bit of after-shave, and goes for a walk. His neighbors are so surprised to see the previously solemn and withdrawn man smiling that many minor mishaps occur, especially when Mr. Hatch waves at them.

At work the next day, Mr. Hatch sits with other workers at lunch and shares some of his candy. On the way home when he stops at his usual newsstand, he speaks to the vendor and finds that the vendor is not feeling very well, so Mr. Hatch minds the newsstand for a while. He performs other acts of kindness which never previously would have occurred to him, all the time wondering about his mysterious friend who sent him the candy. That evening Mr. Hatch bakes brownies and when the smell carries throughout the neighborhood an impromptu picnic is organized, during which Mr. Hatch plays his harmonica.

Things keep getting better for Mr. Hatch until the awful day when the postman returns to say that the precious package had been delivered to Mr. Hatch by mistake. Quickly Mr. Hatch reverts to his old habits and isolation, but this time the neighbors notice, and when they find out about the package, they all come to Mr. Hatch's house with gifts and messages of love.

The illustrations are colored pencil and, at the beginning, are as precise and drab as Mr. Hatch's early life. The page where the package is opened brings the first splash of real color. Everything becomes more colorful in the succeeding pages except when Mr. Hatch's package is reclaimed. We then revert to the drab life as does Mr. Hatch for a few pages.

After Reading the Story

Possible Questions and Topics for Discussion

- What changes in the illustrations accompany the changes in Mr. Hatch?

- Why wouldn't the person who sent the package have signed it?

- Would other neighbors and co-workers have reacted the same way Mr. Hatch did to getting such a package and note? Would the children? Have they ever gotten an anonymous package or note?

- People first notice Mr. Hatch is happy because of the way he smiles and waves as well as by the different clothing he puts on. How would people know if someone were feeling happy? Make a list of ways children know that the different people in their class are happy.

- Suggest that the next time children come to class feeling not-so-good about themselves, they notice the first person to realize that they are not happy. What does he or she do about it? What does the child wish he or she had done?

- Sometimes people work, play or sit alone because they want to be alone. Other times they do it because they don't feel welcome with others. How can children tell the difference?

Activities to Enhance Understanding

- Have children keep a journal for a week in which they note unexpected pleasant interactions with others. Have them make note of how each person reacted and put a star beside the interactions that turned out best.

- Have children make a series of drawings that show people making other people feel welcome and unwelcome.

- Make plans to deliver a package and note similar to the one Mr. Hatch received to an adult the children don't know well but who they think would appreciate such a gift. How will they get it delivered without letting the individual know who they are? How will they find out how the person has reacted? Think it through and then do it.

- Make conical containers with looped handles out of wallpaper samples. Fill them with flowers or small candies. Put a nice but anonymous note in each one. Under supervision, have children place them on door handles of people who live near your school.

Isolation and Reaching Out
Across Generations
Selected Bibliography

Christiansen, Candace. *The Mitten Tree*. Fulcrum, 1997. ISBN 1 55591 349 0.

Spinelli, Eileen. *Somebody Loves You, Mr. Hatch*. Simon & Schuster, 1992. ISBN 0 027 86015 9.

Wild, Margaret and Dee Huxley. *Mr. Nick's Knitting*. Voyager, 1994. ISBN 0 152 00116 6.

Families

Julius, the Baby of the World
by Kevin Henkes

Greenwillow, 1990   ISBN 0 688 08944 5

Comments

There are many good books for kids about sibling rivalry but no one does it any better than Kevin Henkes in this book. Henkes introduced Lilly in *Chester's Way* (see page 9). In *Lilly's Purple Plastic Purse*, she comes into full flower. *Julius, the Baby of the World* was issued between the two. Throughout these three books, Lilly remains a strong personality capable of striking fear in the hearts of her foes. She makes a good subject for this book on the arrival of a new baby because of that very ferocity.

Julius, the Baby of the World allows us to go beyond the feelings created by the presence of a new baby in the house to emotions in general and ways to handle them.

Summary

On the cover of the book we see the baby we will later know as Julius sleeping peacefully in his bassinet, unaware of the angry figure that looms above him. Readers of *Chester's Way* and *Lilly's Purple Plastic Purse* will recognize Lilly by her red boots bedecked with stars in spite of her fake glasses and nose.

The title page shows Lilly and Lilly's parents as they are apparently giving her the news that she's about to be a sister. Her father and mother are smiling and her father has his arm around his wife as Lilly reacts joyously, although perhaps not too politely. Her joy continues on the dedication pages where we see her stuffing pillows under her dress as she announces, "Hooray! We're having a baby!" As the story begins we are told how well Lilly treated Julius before he was born, talking and singing to him.

Everything is changed on the next page. Julius has arrived and Lilly is not happy. We are told that she yells at him, pinches his tail (all right, they're really mice) and, in case there's still some doubt, Lilly tells us directly that she is queen and she hates Julius.

Her parents, however, dote on the new baby proclaiming him the baby of the world. Lilly is not convinced. "Disgusting!" she says. Lilly must now share her room with Julius in spite of the signs she has placed on the door. She asks, "After Julius goes away, do I get my room back?"

But Julius is not going anywhere. In a series of pictures at the bottom of the page we watch the baby as he grows, even learning to crawl. Her parents lean over his crib and tell Julius how much they love him and how beautiful he is. They recite the alphabet and count so that he'll grow up to be clever, like Lilly. When her parents are not around, Lilly leans over his crib and recites a garbled alphabet and number sequence.

We are told that her parents are reluctant to leave Lilly and Julius alone together and we see her tormenting him and then having to spend "more time than usual in the uncooperative chair."

Lilly's parents attempt to deal with Lilly. They show and tell her how much they love her, bring her gifts and cater to her whims, but Lilly is unrepentant and adamant. She hates Julius.

The next pages show Lilly aping everything Julius does— blowing bubbles, shaking a rattle and screaming. Although her parents love those things when Julius does them, they are less pleased with Lilly's antics. When Lilly's mother suggests that Lilly tell Julius a story, the one she tells is probably not what her mother has in mind. Probably that's why Lilly has to spend ten minutes in the uncooperative chair that day.

Lilly next takes her case to a higher court. She tells her friends Chester, Wilson and Victor how dreadful babies are. She accosts a pregnant woman on the street and says, "You'll live to regret that bump under your dress." We are told Lilly runs away seven times in one morning and gives a tea party to which Julius is not invited. Her dreams vary from the sublime—in which she controls a fierce cat about to attack Julius—to the frightening in which a gigantic Julius looms over a minuscule Lilly.

Lilly draws a picture of her "entire complete family." In it Lilly stands large and front and center with her parents in the background. Julius is nowhere in sight. Lilly's parents continue to offer her love and new privileges but they also continue to love and admire their son, kissing his wet pink nose, admiring his small black eyes and stroking his sweet white fur. Throughout it all, Lilly's reaction is unchanged. "Disgusting!" she repeats.

Then comes the day which may well be Julius's christening. At any rate, it's a large party given to honor Julius. Lilly stands aloof as her relatives and friends admire Julius. But it's not Lilly this time who says, "Disgusting." It's Cousin Garland, another relative about Lilly's age. She states exactly what Lilly has said many times, "Julius' nose is slimy, his eyes are beady and his fur is not so sweet."

But Lilly is not delighted to have someone agree with her. Instead, her nose twitches, her eyes narrow and her fur stands on end as her tail quivers. She tells Cousin Garland how very wrong she is. Lilly says her brother's nose is shiny, his eyes are sparkly and his fur smells like perfume. Cousin Garland is cowed by Lilly's ferocious announcements. She tries to slink out of the room, but Lilly is not finished with Cousin Garland yet. As Queen, she commands Cousin Garland to watch as she kisses

Julius' nose, admires his eyes and strokes his fur. "Your turn," says Lilly as she hands him over to Cousin Garland. "Kiss! Admire! Stroke!" Cousin Garland does so but Lilly requires more. She makes her repeat loudly, "Julius is the baby of the world."

The last picture shows Lilly and Julius both wearing fake noses and glasses and red boots bedecked with stars.

After Reading the Story

Possible Questions and Topics for Discussion

- Looking at the book together, decide how Lilly feels at each point in the story and what makes her feel that way. List the words describing those feelings and then encourage children to tell about the last time they felt that way and why.

- Lilly is angry and tries several ways to handle that anger. What else could she have done and what might have been the result? Suggest that children make a list of some of the things they do when they are angry. Help them decide which ways of handling anger are more desirable.

Activities to Enhance Understanding

- To give children some practice in finding out how others feel, use an embroidery hoop as an open mirror. A pair of children sit facing each other through the "mirror." One uses facial expression to convey a feeling. The other tries to name the feeling expressed. When he or she has guessed correctly, it is the other person's turn.

- Set up some ways of handling anger in the classroom—pillows to punch, nails to pound, a place to go and say angry things without being heard, people who promise to listen to how angry one is without doing anything about it.

- To help children get some sense of child development, have them bring in and post their own baby pictures. Arrange them chronologically according to the child's age when each picture was taken. Encourage the children to write or tell others about what they could do and what they liked to do at the age they were in the pictures.

- Make a list of things babies need done for them. Which of those activities would the children be able to help do?

- Sometimes a pattern helps for writing. Use a patterned format such as the following: Babies are _____ and _____, but the most important thing about babies is they __ _____. Suggest that children use words and drawings to fill in the blanks. Post the writing and talk about the different feelings people have about babies.

- After sharing a few of these writings, bring it closer to home with this question, "If your family were expecting a new baby, what would be different at your house?"

Thematically Related Stories

There are some other wonderful books on the subject of a new baby in the house:

- Like Lilly, Frances in *A Baby Sister for Frances* by Lillian and Russell Hoban is so angry at how little attention she gets now that the new baby is here that she runs away. Taking up residence under the dining room table, she hears how much her parents miss her. The little boy in *When the New Baby Comes I'm Moving Out* by Martha Alexander has the same idea.

- In *Darcy and Gran Don't Like Babies* by Jane Cutler, the grandmother is the one who saves the day. She speaks frankly to the little girl who has to deal with the new baby in the family. Everyone else denies her feelings but Gran takes them seriously. Not only that, she takes those feelings one step further, grumbling herself about the babies they see on the street.

- Look together at Jan Ormerod's *101 Things to Do with a Baby*. These wonderful, simple illustrations and the text may help children see some of the delightful things about a baby. *Oh, Baby* by Sara Bonnett Stein may be even more useful for these purposes since it uses photographs of babies to explain what they can do at different stages of development.

- *Peter's Chair* by Ezra Jack Keats may have been around a long time but it is timeless in its gentle story about a little boy who resents the new baby's usurping of his favorite chair even if he can no longer fit in it.

- Mother is napping and the whole family gets involved in trying to figure out *What Baby Wants* by Phyllis Root and Jill Barton. Of course, it's the baby's smart brother who figures it out.

- In Tomie dePaola's *The Baby Sister*, Tomi is delighted about the new baby's arrival. It's his grandmother who comes to take care of him whom he resents.

The Relatives Came
by Cynthia Rylant
Illustrated by Stephen Gammell

Aladdin, 1993   ISBN 0 689 71738 5

Comments

One of the delights of this exuberant celebration of family is that
the people it features are far from wealthy. Their clothes are ill-
fitting and patched. Their car looks as though it has been
assembled from the remains of many. Their houses would not be
easily placed on the market but their love is first class all the way.

Gammell used his own family for models for this book. He
himself is the man who plays the guitar. His father cuts hair and
his wife takes pictures. From this book we can go on to discuss
extended family, family reunions, shared chores and love.

Summary

The cover illustration extends onto the back cover. A multicolored
car bounces along a dirt road with the luggage precariously
perched on the roof. Indeed, some of it has fallen off unnoticed
by the car's occupants. They are all grinning widely and one boy
is stretched out of the window wildly waving his hand.

The title page shows a packed dilapidated suitcase, a pair of
high top sneakers and a teddy bear. The dedication page shows
a broader expanse of packed luggage, all of which looks much
used and over-stuffed.

On the first page we see them packing the car in the not-
quite-dawn. We are told that the scene is Virginia and they are
leaving just before their grapes are ready to pick. As two adults
pack the car, another is working under the hood of a car. Much
of the body of the car is yellow as is one fender. Two fenders are
green and the roof is red. Later, the text calls the car a station
wagon but it does not look like one. Other heads appear in a

lighted window of the house which is what might be called "a fixer upper." The outside walls and roof of the house have been patched many times and the chimney's collapse seems imminent.

The journey begins on the next page. The text tells us that the old station wagon "smelled like a real car." They've knocked down their own mailbox and one suitcase has fallen off the car already. But they're off in the moonlight down a narrow, winding dirt road.

The next page shows us the terrain through which they travel. The homes that are perched on the mountainside are in the same condition as their own as the little car winds through the country-side. A long flight of rickety stairs goes from the road up a steep cliff to one of the houses for what must be a death defying entrance. The journey is long. We are told that they drive all day and into the night. Fortunately, they have brought their own food—soda pop, boxes of crackers and bologna sandwiches.

It is daylight on the next page so they must have driven all night and they are pulling into the narrator's yard at last, knocking down a fence as they do so. Most of the remaining luggage falls off the car now. The three children running out to meet them are colorfully clad and shod. One boy wears one red shoe and the other foot is barefoot. The little girl carrying a teddy bear is barefoot but the older boy has matching high top sneakers

although his shirt is too small for him. So is that of the boy with the red sneaker. A swing dangling from a tree shows a knot in the rope.

Everyone has emerged from car and house on the next page for what the text tells us is "hugging time." These folks may be short on fashion and looks, but they're long on affection. Arms reach out, clasp and shake. Even the boys are touching, although their fists appear to be clenched. Still, there are smiles on their faces so we can assume that the punching is good-natured. An older man with a cane is more reserved. He is better dressed than the others with a neat bow tie and buttoned shirt. As he comes down the stairs of the house, he shakes hands with another man. Even the dog appears happy to see everyone.

The hugging is not over yet. We see many of them inside the house now as we peer through the windows. The text tells us that there is so much hugging that "you'd have to go through at least four different hugs to get from the kitchen to the front room." This house too needs some repair work as does a toy truck lying in the grass near the house.

Food is being served on the next page. Some children are seated at one table while others serve themselves, buffet-style, from another. In the background some balance plates while others relax and chat. The text tells us that they take turns eating "two or three times around."

It's nighttime in the next scene and all are bedded down all over the house. The nighttime attire is no fancier than the daytime clothing but everyone appears to be settling in all right. One old woman is quite child-like in her sleep—an almost fetal position with her thumb in her mouth. The text tells us, "It was different, going to sleep with all that new breathing in the house."

The next day is an active one. A woman is fixing that toy truck, sitting on the ground beside a boy who watches eagerly. Another child plays with a toy car painted exactly like the family's station wagon. An older man cuts a child's hair although the child looks none too happy about that. He's the only one who fails to look happy, however. Three people are digging what appears to be a new garden. A child holds a hoe but appears to be busy talking to another. A bunch of kids are playing in large cardboard cartons while a small child rides "horse" on a man's back. That man, however, has stopped to talk to some other kids. The text tells us that the relatives stay for weeks and weeks and fix things.

Some are still working on the next page. Two men are fixing the fence they crashed into on arrival. Others have begun a concert. One woman plays bass while another plays fiddle. One man plays a guitar and another plays a banjo. A woman holding a very young baby is eating watermelon with a young child doing the same.

There are signs of an imminent departure on the next page. A few packed suitcases are on the ground near the station wagon and family photos are being taken while a dog cleans up some of the food left from a picnic lunch. It's all over. The station wagon heads off. One suitcase bounces onto the road. It's four in the morning. One woman stands in the yard with two children in their pajamas to say goodbye.

Our vantage point draws back a bit and we see the neatly repaired fence in the background as the car with headlights shining askew heads back to Virginia. The last page shows the car in its own garage. The family which has been dreaming about being home in time to pick their grapes is now dreaming about next summer. We see those grapes, dark and ripe, on the last page of the book.

After Reading the Story

Possible Questions and Topics for Discussion

- Examine the pictures together. Do any people appear in more than one illustration? How many are there altogether?

- Notice details like the fallen suitcases, the broken fence, and trucks. Who breaks what? Who fixes what?

- The people here are all having a wonderful time over a period of weeks, yet no one watches television, talks on the telephone, or goes shopping. What do they do? Which of those things would children enjoy?

Activities to Enhance Understanding

- Have children keep a leisure time journal for a week, keeping track of what their family does to have fun either together or individually.

- A lot of work gets done in this book but everyone seems to have a good time doing that work. Have children make a list of chores that have to be done around their house in a week. With which of those chores could they possibly help? Would the person in charge of those chores have more fun if someone helped? Which chores are the child's responsibility? Would children have more fun if somebody helped? Is there a way to make that happen?

- Make a list of the chores that have to be done in the classroom. Who does them? Could kids do any of them? Figure out a way to make the chores easier for the person in charge of each of them.

- The children in the yard are all playing with objects that use imagination and cost very little money. Make a list of other fun activities that kids could do with no toys at all.

- The family in this book includes many people. Figure out how they could all be related. Have children make a list of their own extended families. Which members do they see a lot? Which ones live far away? Which ones live closest? Ask children whether they visit any of them. Ask if any of their relatives visit them. Discuss how children could keep in touch with relatives they cannot see often.

Thematically Related Stories

- Read Donald Crews' *Bigmama's*. In it, a family makes their yearly trek to the grandparents' country house. They travel by train but the exuberance of being together is much like that in *The Relatives Came*. After reading both books, spend some time comparing plot, illustrations and families.

Through Moon and Stars and Night Skies

by Ann Turner
Illustrated by James Graham Hale

HarperTrophy, 1990   ISBN 0 06 443308 0

Comments

This book is about a foreign adoption. It's a tear-jerker so be prepared for your own tears. (The children will probably be interested but not as moved as adults will be.) There's emphasis on
the fear of the unknown as well and on the ways in which the
new parents help calm those fears.

Summary

The cover of the book shows a very happy child looking out of
a dormer window. A large dog looking equally contented gazes
at the child. A narrow frieze on the title page shows us the
moon, stars and night skies. The dedication page shows a bird
flying from two palm trees toward a deciduous tree.

The first scene in the book shows a woman and child sitting
on the steps of the house. The child sits between the woman's
legs as she balances a teacup in one hand and strokes his hair
with the other. The child holds a toy airplane. Both are barefoot
and a dog looks at them through the screen door. The child begs
to be allowed to tell the story this time of how he came to them.
The mother begins the story by saying that once she was a photograph he held in his hand. But the child shushes her and goes
on to tell us the story.

There was more than one photograph, he tells us, and we see
the photos on one page while the full page illustration shows a
different woman sharing the photographs with the child. The
scene outside the window is Asian and some other children are

playing on the floor with tops. The child says that the photographs showed his new mama and poppa, their red dog, and the white house with a green tree in the front and a room inside with a bed waiting for him. On the bed was a teddy bear quilt.

The next page shows the boy sitting on the floor boards of a motor scooter. A sign shows they are heading to the airport. People and beasts of burden are working in the fields as they pass. The child says that he was afraid of flying, of the night, and of the new things.

We see the huge plane from the child's point of view in the next picture and then we see the child sitting cross-legged in the seat. A woman beside him reads a book. He says that he flew all day and all night but did not sleep because he was afraid. He kept the photograph in his hand all the way.

The arrival comes on the next page. A man and woman kneel on the floor, their arms stretched out toward the boy. He says they both cried. He was still afraid, he says, of them and of new things. His mother holds the photograph now as the car draws up in front of the house. The child leans forward from his car seat and points to the house. He knew it was his house.

The tree in front of the house takes center stage in the next picture and we are told that they stopped and picked a leaf from the tree and put it in the boy's hand.

Inside, the room was strange and the child cried when they tried to put him down. It was the dog who made everything all right by rushing up to lick his hand. Smiles began then.

The father takes the child upstairs and they rock in the chair by the window. The boy is holding the pictures again. There's a dog bone on the floor. On the next page the boy is in bed under the teddy bear quilt. They have kissed him and sung to him and he is not so afraid any more.

After Reading the Story

Possible Questions and Topics for Discussion

• After reading the book, look together at those trees on the dedication page and ask if anyone has any suggestions as to why they are there. Some children may be able to see the bird as similar to the child flying from the land of palm trees to the new place.

• Notice the ways in which the new parents helped prepare the child for leaving the familiar to go to a new place. What else might they have done (tape recordings, sending him a toy, etc.)?

• It may be possible to talk with some children about their memories of coming to a new country and maybe even to a new family.

• Talk about some ways in which people seeing that child might have known that he was afraid.

• This family adopted a child from another land. Find out more about adoption and foster families. You may be treading on sensitive ground here so step carefully and make sure everyone is comfortable with such a discussion or has help handling it.

Thematically Related Stories

• Read some other books about families, friends and fears listed on the next page. Compare the ways in which each person expresses his fears and the ways in which those fears are conquered or at least assuaged.

- The little boy in *Gila Monsters Meet You at the Airport* by Marjorie Sharmat has some of the same feelings as the child in *Through Moon and Stars and Night Skies*. He is afraid of the new place he's moving to, but at least he's moving with his whole family instead of all alone. And he knows the language.

- In Kathryn Lasky's *Lunch Bunnies,* illustrated by Marylin Hafner, Clyde is also very frightened. He's about to go to first grade but it is not the classroom he's afraid of—it's the lunch room. His brother's stories about it have scared him half to death.

- The little girl in Dolores Johnson's book *What Will Mommy Do When I'm at School?* projects her fears onto her mother. Surely her mother will be scared and lonely and miss her too much. She'd better not go. Her father tries to reassure her but it's her mother who can best allay those fears.

- Faye Gibbons and Erick Ingraham's *Night in the Barn* portrays a group of friends electing to sleep in the barn. Once darkness falls, some of them are not too sure this was a good plan. *Slumber Party!* by Judith Caseley has a sleep-over in the house but the children scare themselves just the same.

- Sheila Rae in *Sheila Rae, The Brave* by Kevin Henkes claims to be afraid of nothing but then she gets lost and finds out what she does fear.

- The little girl in *Thunder Cake* by Patricia Polacco is afraid of the coming storm. Her grandmother helps by giving her lots to do as the storm approaches. By the time it arrives they're having too much fun to be afraid.

I'll Fix Anthony
by Judith Viorst
Illustrated by Arnold Lobel

Aladdin, 1969   ISBN 0 689 70761 4

Comments

This is a book of plotted revenge in which the younger brother imagines himself at a more powerful age being able to get even with his big brother. Although the idea of revenge may not be a comfortable one for adults, it is a fairly realistic one in the mind of a powerless younger brother. Viorst uses exaggeration and humor to make her points.

Lobel's illustrations are without background; the characters stand against white space, emphasizing the fact that it's the relationship between the two boys that matters. The book can lead to discussions and activities about sibling rivalry and about power and its abuses.

Summary

The cover shows our triumphant younger brother dancing on the back of the defeated Anthony. Anthony looks weak and helpless. On the title page our hero sits astride a large horse. A dog runs along side. Both the horse and the dog appear to be ready to bite Anthony. On the dedication page, Anthony tumbles from his bicycle as our narrator rides ahead no-hands. His dog looks on with approval.

Reality returns, however, in the four vignettes spread across the first two pages. In the first, Anthony sits on a pillow on the floor. A pile of thick books stands at his right and he is smiling as he reads. Behind him stands our narrator clutching a book. We are told that his brother Anthony can read now but won't read to him and we see Anthony chasing him away. Anthony won't play checkers with him either, even though our narrator allows Anthony to wear his Snoopy sweat shirt.

Their mother has tried to reassure our narrator that his brother really loves him deep down inside, but Anthony says that deep down inside he thinks his brother stinks.

The transformation begins on the next page. We see our narrator looking determined and just a bit nasty as he stands alone framed against a black page. From this point on, our narrator relates the delicious vindication he imagines will occur when he becomes six. Of course, in our narrator's imagination, all roles will reverse at that point.

Anthony will stay the same size, or maybe even grow smaller during the intervening years. A dog will follow our narrator home when he is six and will be faithful to him, biting Anthony when he approaches. Anthony will fall victim to a series of illnesses and our narrator will enjoy all sorts of activities without him. Physical achievements will leave our narrator beating Anthony every time. And reading? Our narrator will be reading the *New York Times* when he is six, able to discuss the election intelligently while Anthony is stuck reading an ABC book.

Apparently the ability to stand on one's head has been a bone of contention because our narrator will be able to stand on his head withstanding all sorts of tortures while Anthony will collapse almost immediately. Sharpening pencils will be a breeze for our narrator as will the ability to swim and dive. Anthony, of course, will be stuck with unsharpened pencils and, even worse, he'll sink when he tries to swim.

Anthony will be much smaller and we now learn that that's because he will have eaten jelly beans and root beer instead of the vegetables in the diet of our narrator. Getting his sneakers down from a high shelf that he cannot reach will be a problem for Anthony. Our narrator will, of course, be able to reach them but won't do so unless Anthony says "Please." Our narrator's math abilities will be amazing while Anthony will have to count on his fingers. Even a head start in a footrace won't help Anthony.

Friends will be legion in number for our narrator who will spend lots of time talking to them on the telephone and sleeping over at their houses. Anthony, of course, will stay home friendless.

Telling time, distinguishing left from right and being able to tell one's complete address have apparently been a problem for our narrator but they won't be when he's six.

Our narrator will, reluctantly, rescue Anthony when he is lost. We see Anthony shivering on a remote snow-covered mountain while a well-clad and equipped narrator approaches.

Our narrator will bravely face a doctor's examination including shots while Anthony will quiver under the blankets. Losing one's baby teeth is a mark of maturity that will not happen for Anthony no matter how much he wiggles them.

Reality reappears at the end of the book as Anthony chases our narrator out of the playroom, but his resolve is unaltered. When he's six, everything will change.

After Reading the Story

Possible Questions and Topics for Discussion

- After enjoying the book together, decide which of the imagined role reversals predicted by our narrator are possible.

- If Anthony is now six, how old is the narrator? How old, then, will Anthony be when our narrator is six?

- Retell the book together from Anthony's point of view. Use as many of the events in the story as possible.

- Make a list of the skills the narrator apparently has not mastered yet. Some children may be willing to admit that some of those tasks are difficult for them now. What can they do to master them? Are they doing those things?

- Make a list of the disadvantages of having older siblings. Make another list of disadvantages of being the oldest sibling. Make a list of disadvantages of being the only child in a family. Make a list of the advantages of each of those roles. Encourage children to imagine what it would be like to be in each role.

Activities to Enhance Understanding

- After reading the book, discuss what problems Anthony and his little brother experience. Role-play a conversation between Anthony and our narrator in which some of their problems are addressed.

- Have children make lists of problems they see between themselves and their siblings. Role-play conversations between class members and their bigger or younger siblings in which some of their problems are addressed.

Thematically Related Stories

- Read *Noisy Nora* by Rosemary Wells. Nora lacks attention from her parents in this very busy family. A rhyming patterned text tells how Nora has to wait no matter what she needs or wants. Like Frances in *A Baby Sister for Frances* (see page 65), Nora runs away to a lair under the dining room table. Use the pattern of *Noisy Nora* to write a class poem about children in the classroom having to wait for attention.

- Patty Jean, in *Now I Will Never Leave the Dinner Table* by Jane Read Martin and Roz Chast, is being cared for by an older sister who insists that she eat all her spinach before leaving the table. Patty Jean sits and, like Anthony, plans her revenge.

- Stanley, in *Stanley and Rhoda* by Rosemary Wells, exacts a much more subtle and far less violent revenge on his pesky younger sister.

Families

Selected Bibliography

Alexander, Martha. *When the New Baby Comes I'm Moving Out.* Dial, 1992. ISBN 0 140 54723 1.

Caseley, Judith. *Slumber Party!* Greenwillow, 1996. ISBN 0 688 14015 7.

Crews, Donald. *Bigmama's.* Greenwillow, 1992. ISBN 0 688 09950 5.

Cutler, Jane. *Darcy and Gran Don't Like Babies.* Scholastic, 1993. ISBN 0 590 72126 7.

dePaola, Tomie. *The Baby Sister.* Putnam, 1996. ISBN 0 399 22908 6.

Gibbons, Faye and Erick Ingraham. *Night in the Barn.* Morrow, 1995. ISBN 0 688 13326 6.

Henkes, Kevin. *Julius, the Baby of the World.* Greenwillow, 1990. ISBN 0 688 08944 5.

-----. *Lilly's Purple Plastic Purse.* Greenwillow, 1996. ISBN 0 688 12897 1.

-----. *Sheila Rae, The Brave.* Mulberry, 1987. ISBN 0 688 14738 0.

Hoban, Lillian and Russell Hoban. *A Baby Sister for Frances.* Harpercrest, 1993. ISBN 0 06 022336 7.

Johnson, Dolores. *What Will Mommy Do When I'm at School?* Simon, 1990. ISBN 0 02 747845 9.

Keats, Ezra Jack. *Peter's Chair.* Viking, 1998. ISBN 0 670 88064 7.

Lasky, Kathryn. *Lunch Bunnies.* Little, 1996. ISBN 0 316 51525 6.

Martin, Jane Read and Roz Chast. *Now I Will Never Leave the Dinner Table.* HarperCollins, 1996. ISBN 0 06 024794 0.

Ormerod, Jan. *101 Things to Do with a Baby.* Mulberry, 1994. ISBN 0 688 12770 3.

Polacco, Patricia. *Thunder Cake.* Philomel, 1990. ISBN 0 399 22231 6.

Root, Phyllis, and Jill Barton. *What Baby Wants*. Candlewick, 1998. ISBN 0 763 60207 8.

Rylant, Cynthia. *The Relatives Came*. Aladdin, 1993. ISBN 0 689 71738 5.

Sharmat, Marjorie. *Gila Monsters Meet You at the Airport*. Aladdin, 1980. ISBN 0 689 71383 5.

Stein, Sara Bonnett. *Oh, Baby*. Walker, 1995. ISBN 0 802 77464 4.

Turner, Ann. *Through Moon and Stars and Night Skies*. HarperTrophy, 1990. ISBN 0 06 443308 0.

Viorst, Judith. *I'll Fix Anthony*. Aladdin, 1969. ISBN 0 689 70761 4.

Wells, Rosemary. *Noisy Nora*. Puffin, 1973. ISBN 0 14 054674 X.

-----. *Stanley and Rhoda*. Dial, 1981. ISBN 0 8037 7995 X.

Working Together

Officer Buckle & Gloria
by Peggy Rathmann

Putnam, 1995   ISBN 0 399 22616 8

Comments

This funny Caldecott Award winning book deals with safety as well as with sharing the limelight and jealousy. If safety awareness is a part of your curriculum, don't miss the opportunity to approach it through this delightful book.

Here we will deal with the subject of safety only as far as unsafe behavior affects the group. However, our focus is on the relationship between Officer Buckle and Gloria. Although Gloria is a dog, her relationship with Officer Buckle is one of true friendship. Each is less interesting and less powerful without the other. Rathmann's large, cartoon-style illustrations are perfect for this book which is full of slapstick humor.

Summary

On the cover, a perturbed Officer Buckle stands in the spotlight in front of a large group of children. The border contains stars bearing tiny illustrations and even tinier print. Above the title, which appears on a banner, is Gloria, a smooth-haired dog in the middle of a backward flip. On the end papers of the book, the stars from the cover are more legible. Each bears an image of Gloria acting out a different safety rule—or the consequence of ignoring that rule. Most of the rules are good, sensible ones but there's a ringer or two. The star theme appears again on the dedication page. The title in which Gloria gets star billing appears over Officer Buckle, seated at his desk, writing out a series of numbered safety rules.

The spills begin on the first page as an airborne Officer Buckle falls off his swivel chair. A box of tacks is also spilling off the desk. The text tells us that this inspires him to thumbtack a new safety rule to his bulletin board, "Safety Tip #77, Never stand on a swivel chair." We see his bulletin board and can decipher some of his rules.

On the next page we see Officer Buckle at Napville School earnestly reading from a large stack of papers. He stands on a school stage while the children in the audience sleep, play and otherwise ignore him. As Officer Buckle leaves the safety lecture, accidents are in progress all around him. Even the principal is about to fall off a swivel chair, ignoring the warning Officer Buckle has just given at the school. We meet Gloria on the next page and Officer Buckle introduces her to the children. He tells her to sit and she does.

Officer Buckle starts his lecture and we see Gloria imitate his stance on the stage. Yet as he turns toward her, Officer Buckle sees Gloria sitting at attention. The children, however, don't miss the trick.

Officer Buckle announces his next safety tip, "Always wipe up spills before someone slips and falls." Gloria, slightly behind him on the stage, stands on her head, but as he looks back, Officer Buckle sees her just as before. "Never leave a thumbtack where you might sit on it" sends Gloria high into the air, holding her backside. The children laugh loudly. Thinking that it is his impassioned delivery that has gotten the crowd's attention, Officer Buckle delivers the rest of the rules with lots of expression. Gloria is in constant action as he does so. This time the children heed his words and no accidents occur afterward.

Letters from the children of Napville School arrive at Officer Buckle's desk the next day. Each letter bears an illustration of Gloria in action but Officer Buckle credits the kids' imagination for that. Claire's letter is cut in the shape of a star and shows Officer Buckle and Gloria standing with their arms around each other. She says that they make a good team.

Word spreads and now many schools are calling to get Officer Buckle and Gloria to visit their schools. After each performance, Officer Buckle takes Gloria out for ice cream. While he's buying it, we see Gloria signing autographs for the children.

Everything is going very well until a television news team tapes the safety lecture. Gloria's routine when Officer Buckle concludes his presentation with "Do not go swimming during electrical storms" brings the audience to its feet. Still unaware of Gloria's contribution, Officer Buckle is seen bowing humbly.

In the next spread we see Officer Buckle on his couch. His popcorn is spilling onto the floor as a worried Gloria watches him react to the television tape. The next morning Officer Buckle turns down a request to present the safety lecture at Napville School. Gloria goes on alone, but without Officer Buckle she has no routine. Both she and the audience fall asleep and Napville School has its worst accidents ever. Banana pudding spills on the cafeteria floor, the principal falls off the swivel chair, children fall all over the place, a hammer flies through the air.

Letters of protest arrive at the police station but one letter is from Claire. It says, "Gloria missed you yesterday." Amends are made. Gloria kisses Officer Buckle. He pats her on the back and thinks of his best safety tip yet, "Always stick with your buddy."

After Reading the Story

Possible Questions and Topics for Discussion

- Look first at the cover and ask children to describe the way they think each of the characters feels at that moment. Do the same thing for the moment at which Gloria and Officer Buckle have finished their first performance together at Napville School. Do it again at the point where Officer Buckle and Gloria view the tape and when Gloria goes to the school without Officer Buckle. Do it once more for the page where Gloria is licking Officer Buckle's face.

Activities to Enhance Understanding

- When Officer Buckle and Gloria are together, they are more successful and have more fun than when they are apart. Make a list of activities that are best for two people to enjoy together such as checkers, chess, and tennis. Create a series of buddy days in which one hour of the day is spent with a partner. Make sure each child has a different partner each day. Do it for an entire day. Is it easier? Harder? More or less fun?

- Do some experiments comparing activities done alone with the same activity done in pairs. For instance, try some foot races where one person races alone in a timed event, and then, after resting, where two people race as partners in a relay. Is each contestant's time better, worse or the same as when they raced alone? Do the same with a trivia game, homework, and classroom chores.

Thematically Related Stories

- Read other books in which a human and an animal are friends such as *Elizabeth and Larry* by Marilyn Sadler, illustrated by Roger Bollen. Their portrait on the first page sets the tone nicely for this straight-faced outlandish tale with the caption: "Elizabeth and Larry were old friends. Elizabeth was sixty-two and Larry was pushing forty." Larry is an alligator in appearance but a person on the inside. His life with Elizabeth is dignified, comfortable and filled with mutual respect. It's the outside world that gives them trouble. List the ways in which Gloria and Larry are more like humans than animals.

- For a nonfictional look at two disparate creatures who became friends, try *Koko's Kitten* by Francine Patterson and Ronald Cohn. This photo essay tells about the friendship between a gorilla and a kitten. The gorilla, Koko, asked for a kitten and got one. When the kitten died, Koko mourned. The book can lead to a discussion about animals as friends or friendships between animals.

- You can go even farther into the idea of disparate friendships by using Leo Lionni's fable *Little Blue & Little Yellow*. This simple story of friendship and racism has been a favorite for years. It is told with blobs of color which become the characters. When Little Blue and Little Yellow, two fast friends, are reunited after being apart for a while, they hug each other and become green whereupon they are each rejected by their own families. You can use it to discuss the fears of being different and the fear of differences in other people. Children may be willing to tell about a person who looked different and frightened them. You can then talk about reasonable and unreasonable fears.

Yard Sale
by James Stevenson

Greenwillow, 1996   ISBN 0 688 14126 9

Comments

Some early readers will be able to read this book on their own. It's funny and, although the characters are not above using some fast talking to make their deals, in the end the friendships are secure and fairness prevails. Stevenson's touch is light in this and in all the Mud Flat books, and although his characters may resemble animals in appearance, they are more like ourselves than any animal.

Summary

With this book, Stevenson further explores the community he created in several other books (see book list on page 93) in which a motley crew of woodland animals act within their community. Each book in this series contains short, easy to read chapters and small watercolor illustrations.

In *Yard Sale* we find Simsbury, a creature who might be a groundhog, watching various items being carried through the woods. We learn, as he does, that there is about to be a yard sale and everyone in Mud Flat is gathering unwanted items for the sale. Simsbury goes off to find his own items to sell as we follow his neighbors to the yard sale.

The first items do not look too promising: a couple of picture frames, a cracked teacup, an old book, and a broken hockey stick. Delphina, a pig, questions the broken hockey stick but Crocker, a crocodile, insists that it will be ideal for a very small hockey player.

Crocker has an alarm clock for sale and he immediately begins hawking it as something very rare and special. Further questioning by Henry, the raccoon, reveals that this is a silent alarm clock and that Crocker is asking fifty cents for it. Henry notices that the clock has no hands but Crocker says that if it did, he would have to charge more for it. Furthermore the clock is pre-wound so you never have to wind it. That's good enough for Henry. He buys the clock and hurries home with it because, as Crocker has warned, someone else might want to steal it. Crocker is encouraged by his success and is off to sell his necktie that he swears was once worn by George Washington.

All this has been observed by two butterflies who are watching from afar. They have nothing to sell because they own nothing, so they go off to smell the honeysuckle.

Simsbury, in the meantime, searches for treasures in his attic to sell at the yard sale. He's surprised at how much junk he has in his attic and decides this is the time to get rid of it. Of course, he can't sell that old bike with the twisted frame and flat tires because he might one day want to go for a spin. The picture postcards hold lovely pictures too good to sell and an hour later we find Simsbury playing a three string guitar and singing songs from long ago. Fortunately for us, the yard sale continues. April has a comb and Naomi is interested. April, though, says that this is a comb she loves, owned first by her grandmother and then by her mother. It would be hard to sell at any price but when Naomi offers fifteen cents she gets the comb.

Beth sells a tattered footstool to Matthew for five cents and later sees Matthew sitting on it. Matthew says he loves that footstool and does not know how he ever got along without it. Beth offers him five cents to get it back but Matthew says it's worth more now because it is older and gets ten cents for it from Beth. The sales go on. Margaret sells one end of an accordion to Nick while Clyde is selling the other end to Myrna. Margaret's advice to Nick and Myrna? Share!

Simsbury arrives at the yard sale at dusk carrying an old top hat. The yard sale is over but he's not too late for the party and, fortunately, he has a top hat to wear for it. At the party, Nick and Myrna have apparently learned to share because they play their accordion. Crocker offers to buy back the alarm clock from Henry but Henry insists that he likes it. Matthew and Beth share the orange footstool while they eat their ice cream and cake and Simsbury plays some old songs as everyone walks home.

After Reading the Story

Possible Questions and Topics for Discussion

- Follow each item sold at the yard sale. Who sells it? What did the seller use to sell it? Who buys it? Does it change hands again? Who got the best of the deal? Chart the answers.

Item	Who Sold It?	What Was Claimed About It?	Who Bought It?	Outcome
Footstool	Beth	Came from a castle	Matthew	Beth bought it back

- Look at each sale in the chart. Which sales were not fair? Why? Make a list of rules for fair negotiation.

- Crocker makes claims for all his wares. Are any of the claims he makes fair? What does he do about that later? Why does Crocker decide to give Henry back his money for the clock? How might Henry have felt when he bought the clock? How might he have felt about that clock the next day if he had not gotten his money back?

- Notice the way different characters in the book feel about their possessions. Simsbury can't bear to part with most of his. The butterflies have no possessions.

- The characters in the book negotiate the prices of the items they have for sale. How do they decide on the price for each item?

Activities to Enhance Understanding

- Role-play a fair and polite negotiation and an argumentative one. Other members of the class should watch the role play and notice what happened. Did body language change during the respectful and the argumentative negotiations? How did the players show respect? How did they show anger or disrespect?

- How do children feel about their own stuff? Which of it might look like junk to someone else? Have them make a list of the articles they have that they want to keep and another list of the items they have that they might be willing to sell or trade. Children can make advertisements for the items they are willing to sell or trade.

- Place each character's name on a card. Scatter the cards on a bulletin board. Put yarn between the names of any characters that interact.

- Bring in articles for a yard sale and negotiate. Afterwards, have children discuss ways in which they were like or unlike any character in the story.

Thematically Related Stories

- Read other books in the series about Mud Flat: *Heat Wave at Mud Flat, Mud Flat April Fool, The Mud Flat Mystery, The Mud Flat Olympics, Mud Flat Spring* (soon to be published). Do any of the characters in this book show up in any of the other books? Add any new characters from these books to the bulletin board and add appropriate pieces of connecting yarn.

- After you've read most or all of the Mud Flat books, are there any conclusions children can draw about the characters of Mud Flat? Is the Mud Flat community in any way like your classroom community?

Working Together

Selected Bibliography

Lionni, Leo. *Little Blue & Little Yellow.* Mulberry, 1995. ISBN 0 688 13285 5.

Patterson, Francine and Ronald Cohn. *Koko's Kitten.* Scholastic, 1987. ISBN 0 590 44425 5.

Rathmann, Peggy. *Officer Buckle & Gloria.* Putnam, 1995. ISBN 0 399 22616 8.

Sadler, Marilyn. *Elizabeth and Larry.* Simon & Schuster, 1990. ISBN 0 671 77817 X.

Stevenson, James. *Heat Wave at Mud Flat.* Greenwillow, 1997. ISBN 0 688 14205 2.

-----. *Mud Flat April Fool.* Greenwillow, 1998. ISBN 0 688 15164 7.

-----. *The Mud Flat Mystery.* Greenwillow, 1997. ISBN 0 688 14965 0.

-----. *The Mud Flat Olympics.* Greenwillow, 1994. ISBN 0 688 12924 2.

-----. *Mud Flat Spring.* In press.

-----. *Yard Sale.* Greenwillow, 1996. ISBN 0 688 14126 9.

Afterword

THESE STORIES REPRESENT our choices for good books about interpersonal relationships and our suggestions for ways to use them in the classroom to stimulate discussions and activities about how people treat one another. We hope you won't stop with these activities, however.

Because all of these are good strong books, their contributions can extend far beyond this part of the curriculum. All of the books, by their very nature, are rich in material for increasing knowledge and facility in the language arts and many touch upon areas of math, science, health and social studies. *Julius, the Baby of the World,* for example, can be used as a springboard for activities about growth and development. *The Relatives Came* might lead to mapping activities or a look at car travel as compared to other methods of transportation. Even the animal characters themselves in many of the books can lead to science activities in which the attributes of mice, frogs, toads and owls are researched and compared.

By using these books and others like them to step into other areas of the curriculum, we show children that learning is not discrete. It does not fit neatly into a little box. The best books give us knowledge but they also make us want to know more. Good literature opens doors to further reading and learning.

About the Authors

Carol Otis Hurst

A former teacher and school librarian, Carol Otis Hurst is a nationally-known storyteller, language arts consultant, columnist and author of books on children's literature.

Two columns by Carol appear each month in *Teaching K–8 Magazine*: "Teaching in the Library" and "Kids' Books." She is the author of twelve professional books for teachers, several of which are published by SRA/McGraw, and is one of three major authors of the DLM Early Childhood Program, which has been widely adopted in preschools and kindergartens in the United States and Canada. Three recent books by Carol Otis Hurst have been published by Linworth Publishers. They are *Using Picture Books in the Upper Grades; Using Literature in the Middle School Curriculum;* and *Open Books: A Guide to Literature in the Early Grades*.

Carol, who is the mother of two daughters and the grand-mother of two grandsons, currently lives in Westfield, Mass-achusetts.

Rebecca Otis

Rebecca Otis is the co-author of several books for teachers, including *In Times Past: An Encyclopedia for Integrating U.S. History with Literature in Grades 3–8; Picturing Math: Using Picture Books in the Math Curriculum;* and *Using Literature in the Middle School Curriculum*. She's the webmaster of "Carol Hurst's Children's Literature Site," which you can find at http://www.carolhurst.com, and she publishes the quarterly *Carol Hurst's Children's Literature Newsletter*.

Rebecca lives in Colrain, Massachusetts and is the parent of two boys who are students in a Responsive Classroom school.

Other Books in
The Small Book Series

Off to a Good Start: Launching the School Year
Excerpts from the Responsive Classroom Newsletter

Nine of the most frequently requested Responsive Classroom newsletter articles featuring ideas for building a strong and caring learning community. Useful at any time in the school year, this book includes strategies for:

- Establishing rules
- Building a sense of group
- Making lunch a positive experience
- Introducing and caring for materials
- Displaying students' work
- Involving parents

Familiar Ground: Traditions that Build School Community
by Libby Woodfin

Familiar Ground shows how Greenfield Center School, Northeast Foundation for Children's K–8 laboratory school, uses traditions like all-school meetings, mixed-age games, and partner lunches to create a strong sense of whole-school community. Descriptions of the traditions are accompanied by guidelines for implementing these traditions in other settings.

For a complete catalog of resources
or to receive our free newsletter
published quarterly, contact us at:

The Responsive Classroom
Northeast Foundation for Children
85 Avenue A, Suite 204, P.O. Box 718
Turners Falls, MA 01376-0718

Phone: 800-360-6332 Fax: 877-206-3952

www.responsiveclassroom.org

Date Due

OC 7 '06			

BRODART, CO.   Cat. No. 23-233-003   Printed in U.S.A.

Please remember that this is a library book,
and that it belongs only temporarily to each
person who uses it. Be considerate. Do
not write in this, or any, library book.